City, Project and Equity

From Languages and Appropriations to Forms of Regulation

City, Project and Equity

From Languages and Appropriations to Forms of Regulation

Organizers: Wilson Florio • Fabio Ramazzini Bechara • Felipe Chiarello de Souza Pinto

Alicia Novick
Andresa Ledo Marques
Angélica Tanus Benatti Alvim
Axel Föller
Bernhard Johannes Fichtner
Bianka Mieskes
Carlos Leite
Daniela Getlinger
Elisabete Castanheira
Eunice Helena S. Abascal
Federica Maietti
Felipe Corres Melachos
Fernando de Oliveira Domingues Ladeira
Ingrid Hötte Ambrogi
Irene Patrícia Nohara
João Clemente de S. Neto
Jörg Schröder
Julia Motte-Baumvol
Luca Rossato
Matteo Finco
Natalia Feld
Orlando Villas Bôas Filho
Rosana M. P.B. Schwartz
Solange Teles da Silva
Tarin Cristino Frota Mont'Alverne

ALMEDINA
BRASIL

Rio de Janeiro, 2024

City, Project and Equity

ALMEDINA é uma empresa do Grupo Editorial Alta Books (STARLIN ALTA EDITORA E CONSULTORIA LTDA).

ISBN: 978-85-8493-703-5

Impresso no Brasil – 1ª Edição, 2024– Edição revisada conforme o Acordo Ortográfico da Língua Portuguesa de 2009.

Dados Internacionais de Catalogação na Publicação (CIP)
(Câmara Brasileira do Livro, SP, Brasil)

City, project and equity : from languages and appropriations to forms of regulation / coordenação Wilson Florio, Fabio Ramazzini Bechara, Felipe Chiarello de Souza Pinto. -- São Paulo : Almedina, 2024.

Vários autores
ISBN 978-85-8493-703-5

1. Cidadania 2. Cidades - Administração 3. Direito imobiliário - Leis e legislação - Brasil 4. Exclusão social 5. Mobilidade urbana 6. Urbanismo - Aspectos sociais I. Florio, Wilson. II. Bechara, Fabio Ramazzini. III. Pinto, Felipe Chiarello de Souza.

24-196748 CDD-307.76

Índices para catálogo sistemático:

1. Cidades : Sociologia urbana 307.76

Eliane de Freitas Leite - Bibliotecária - CRB 8/8415

Grupo Editorial Alta Books

Produção Editorial: Grupo Editorial Alta Books
Diretor Editorial: Anderson Vieira
Editora-Chefe: Manuella Santos de Castro
Editor Pleno: Aurélio Nogueira
Vendas Governamentais: Cristiane Mutüs
Gerência Comercial: Claudio Lima

Assistente Editorial: Andreza Moraes
Revisão: João Paulo Guterres
Diagramação: Almedina e Aurélio Corrêa

ALTA BOOKS
GRUPO EDITORIAL

Rua Viúva Cláudio, 291 – Bairro Industrial do Jacaré
CEP: 20.970-031 – Rio de Janeiro (RJ)
Tels.: (21) 3278-8069 / 3278-8419
www.altabooks.com.br – altabooks@altabooks.com.br
Ouvidoria: ouvidoria@altabooks.com.br

Editora
afiliada à:

ASSOCIADO

ABOUT THE ORGANIZERS

Wilson Florio
Livre-Docente pela Universidade Estadual de Campinas (UNICAMP). Doutor e Mestre em Arquitetura e Urbanismo pela Universidade de São Paulo (USP). Professor Adjunto da Faculdade de Arquitetura e Urbanismo da Universidade Presbiteriana Mackenzie e Professor Associado do Instituto de Artes da Universidade Estadual de Campinas. Arquiteto e Urbanista.
Full Professor from Campinas State University (UNICAMP). PhD and Master in Architecture and Urban Planning from the University of São Paulo (USP). Adjunct Professor of the Faculty of Architecture and Urban Planning of the Mackenzie Presbyterian University and Associate Professor of the Arts Institute of Campinas State University. Architect and Urban Planner.

Fabio Ramazzini Bechara
Doutor em Direito Processual Penal pela Universidade de São Paulo. Mestre em Direito Processual Penal pela Pontifícia Universidade Católica de São Paulo. Coordenador do Programa de Pós-Graduação Strictu Sensu de Direito Político e Econômico da Universidade Presbiterana Mackenzie. Professor dos Programas de Graduação e Pós-Graduação de Mestrado/ /Doutorado em Direito Político e Econômico da Faculdade de Direito da Universidade Presbiteriana Mackenzie. Professor da Escola Superior do Ministério Público do Estado de São Paulo. Promotor de Justiça no Estado de São Paulo desde 1996.

PhD in Criminal Procedure Law from the University of São Paulo. Master's in Criminal Procedural Law from the Pontifical Catholic University of São Paulo. Coordinator of the Strictu Sensu Postgraduate Program in Political and Economic Law at Mackenzie Presbyterian University. Professor of the Undergraduate and Postgraduate Masters/Doctorate Programs in Political and Economic Law at the Mackenzie Presbyterian University Law School. Professor at the Higher School of the Public Prosecutor's Office of the State of São Paulo. Prosecutor in the State of São Paulo since 1996.

Felipe Chiarello de Souza Pinto

Possui mestrado e doutorado em Direito pela Pontifícia Universidade Católica de São Paulo. Pró-Reitor de Pesquisa e Pós-Graduação e Professor Titular da Faculdade de Direito e do Programa de Mestrado e Doutorado em Direito Político e Econômico da Universidade Presbiteriana Mackenzie e Membro da Academia Mackenzista de Letras.

He holds a master's degree and a doctorate in law from the Pontifical Catholic University of São Paulo. He is the Dean of Research and Postgraduate Studies and Full Professor at the Faculty of Law and the Master's and Doctorate Program in Political and Economic Law at Mackenzie Presbyterian University and a member of the Mackenzie Academy of Letters.

ABOUT THE AUTHORS

Alicia Novick

Doutora em História e Mestre em Investigação Histórica (UDESA). Mestre em Urbanismo e Planejamento Territorial (Instituto de Urbanismo de Paris, Paris XII). Diretora do Programa de Mestrado e Doutorado em Estudos Urbanos (UNGS). Professora e pesquisadora na Universidade General Sarmiento (UNGS) e na Universidade de Buenos Aires (UBA). Arquiteta.
PhD. in History and Magister in Historical Research (UDESA). Master in Urban Planning and Territorial Planning (Institute of Urbanism of Paris, Paris XII). Director of the Master's and Doctorate Program in Urban Studies (UNGS). Professor and researcher at the General Sarmiento University (UNGS) and in the University of Buenos Aires (UBA). Architect.

Andresa Ledo Marques

Doutora em Arquitetura e Urbanismo pela Universidade Presbiteriana Mackenzie e Doktorin der Ingenieurwissenschaften pela Gottfried Wilhelm Leibniz Universität Hannover. Arquiteta e Urbanista.
Doctor in Architecture and Urbanism by the Universidade Presbiteriana Mackenzie and Doktorin der Ingenieurwissenschaften by the Gottfried Wilhelm Leibniz Universität Hannover. Master in Architecture and Urban Planning from Mackenzie Presbyterian University. Architect and Urban Planner.

Angélica Tanus Benatti Alvim

Doutora e Mestre em Arquitetura e Urbanismo pela Universidade de São Paulo (USP). Professora Titular da Faculdade de Arquitetura e Urbanismo e do Programa de Pós-Gradução em Arquitetura e Urbanismo

da Universidade Presbiteriana Mackenzie. Coordenadora do Grupo de Pesquisa Urbanismo contemporâneo: redes, sistemas e processos. Bolsista Produtividade CNPq 1 D.
Doctor and Master in Architecture and Urban Planning from the University of São Paulo (USP). Full Professor at the Faculty of Architecture and Urban Planning and Postgraduate Program in Architecture and Urban Planning at Universidade Presbiteriana Mackenzie. Coordinator of the Contemporary Urbanism Research Group: networks, systems and processes. Productivity Scholarship CNPq 1 D.

Axel Föller
Professor da Universidad Alanus de Artes y Ciencias Sociales. Departamento de Educacão com Doutorado como no Departamento de Ciências Matemáticas e Tecnologia (IMT).
Professor at the Alanus University of Arts and Social Sciences. Department of Education with a PhD in the Department of Mathematical Sciences and Technology (IMT).

Bernhard Johannes Fichtner
Possui doutorado em Pädagogik pela Pädagogische Hochschule Münster. É livre docente pela Universidade de Siegen (1989). Atualmente é professor titular concursado da Universität Siegen (Siegener Zentrumfür Kindheits-, Jugend-und Biografiefor), sendo ainda colaborador junto à Universidade Alanus de Arte e Sociedade. E Membro de corpo editorial da Kulturen des Lernens.
He holds a doctorate in Pädagogik from the Pädagogische Hochschule Münster. He is a full professor at the University of Siegen (1989). He is currently a full professor at the Universität Siegen (Siegener Zentrumfür Kindheits-, Jugend-und Biografiefor) and a collaborator at the Alanus University of Art and Society. He is also a member of the editorial board of Kulturen des Lernens.

Bianka Mieskes
Docente em Escultura, Instalação e novas mídias na Alanus University of Arts and Social Sciences — Bonn, Alemanha, examinadora de teses de licenciatura e mestrado. Docente na Artefact, Freie Kunstschule, Bonn, Alemanha. Docente na Alanus Werkhaus, Bonn, Alemanha.
Docent in Sculpture, Installation, and New Media at Alanus University of Arts and Social Sciences, Bonn, Germany, Bachelor and Master thesis examiner. Docent at Artefact, Freie Kunstschule, Bonn, Germany. Docent at Alanus Werkhaus, Bonn, German.

Carlos Leite

Pós Doutor pela CalPoly (EUA); Doutor e Mestre pela FAU-USP; Diretor da Faculdade de Arquitetura e Urbanismo da Universidade Presbiteriana Mackenzie e Professor do Programa de Pós-Graduação em Arquitetura e Urbanismo da mesma Instituição. Arquiteto e Urbanista.

Post Doctorate from CalPoly (USA). Director of the Faculty of Architecture and Urbanism at Universidade Presbiteriana Mackenzie (since 2023) and Professor of the Postgraduate Program in Architecture and Urban Planner at the same institution.

Daniela Getlinger

Doutora e Mestre em Arquitetura e Urbanismo pela Universidade Presbiteriana Mackenzie. M.Arch.II pela University of California, Los Angeles (UCLA). Professora da Faculdade de Arquitetura e Urbanismo da Universidade Presbiteriana Mackenzie. Arquiteta e Urbanista.

PhD and Master in Architecture and Urban Planning from Mackenzie Presbyterian University. Master from UCLA. Professor at Mackenzie Presbyterian University. Architect and Urban Planner.

Elisabete Castanheira

Doutora e Mestre em Arquitetura e Urbanismo pela Universidade Presbiteriana Mackenzie. Designer pela FAAP – Fundação Armando Álvares Penteado. Professora na Universidade São Francisco (USF) e na Universidade Santo Amaro (UNISA).

PhD and Master in Architecture and Urban Planning from Mackenzie Presbyterian University. Designer by Fundação Armando Álvares Penteado (FAAP). Professor at the São Francisco University (USF) and at the Santo Amaro University (UNISA).

Eunice Helena S. Abascal

Pós Doutora em Urbanismo e Ordenamento Territorial pela Escola Técnica Superior de Arquitectura (ETSAB) da Universidade Politécnica de Catalunha – UPC (Espanha). Doutora em Arquitetura e Urbanismo pela Universidade de São Paulo (USP). Mestre em Comunicação e Letras pela Universidade Presbiteriana Mackenzie. Professora Titular na Faculdade de Arquitetura e Urbanismo da Universidade Presbiteriana Mackenzie. Arquiteta e Urbanista. Bolsista Produtividade CNPq Nível 2.

Post Doctorate in Urban Planning and Territorial Planning by the Superior Technical School of Architecture (ETSAB) of the Polytechnic University of

Catalonia – UPC (Spain). PhD in Architecture and Urban Planning from the University of São Paulo (USP). Master in Communication and Liberal Arts from Mackenzie Presbyterian University. Full Professor at the Faculty of Architecture and Urban Planning at Mackenzie Presbyterian University. Architect and Urban Planner. CNPq Productivity Scholarship Level 2.

Federica Maietti
Doutora em Tecnologia da Arquitetura. Professor Associado ICAR/17 do Departamento de Arquitetura da Universidade de Ferrara. Professor de Projeto Arquitetônico e Pesquisa Arquitetônica II. Membro do Centro Departamental DIAPReM, Centro de Desenvolvimento de Procedimentos Automáticos Integrados para a Restauração de Monumentos. Arquiteta.
PhD in Technology of Architecture. Associate Professor ICAR/17 at the Department of Architecture of the University of Ferrara. Professor of Architectural Design and Architectural Survey II. Member of the DIAPReM Departmental Center, Center for the Development of Integrated Automatic Procedures for the Restoration of Monuments. Architect.

Felipe Corres Melachos
Mestre em Arquitetura e Urbanismo pela Universidade Presbiteriana Mackenzie. Doutor em Arquitetura e Urbanismo pela mesma Universidade com dupla titulação pela Università degli Studi di Ferrara.
Master in Architecture and Urban Planning from Mackenzie Presbyterian University and PhD. in Architecture and Urban Planning from the same University with a double degree from the Univesità degli Studi di Ferrara. Professor at the State University of Campinas (UNICAMP). Architect and Urban Planner.

Fernando de Oliveira Domingues Ladeira
Doutorando em Direito Político e Econômico na Universidade Presbiteriana Mackenzie. Mestre em Direito Político e Econômico pela Universidade Presbiteriana Mackenzie. Especialista em Direito Público pela Escola Paulista de Magistratura. Bacharel em Direito pela Universidade de São Paulo.
PhD candidate in Political and Economic Law at Mackenzie Presbyterian University. Master in Political and Economic Law from Mackenzie Presbyterian University. Specialist in Public Law from Escola Paulista de Magistratura. Bachelor of Laws from the University of São Paulo.

Ingrid Hötte Ambrogi

Doutora em História Social pela Faculdade de Filosofia, Letras e Ciências Humanas, Universidade de São Paulo (FFLCH-USP). Mestre em Psicologia Escolar e do Desenvolvimento Humano (IP-USP). Professora do Programa de Pós-Graduação em Educação, Arte e História da Cultura e do Curso de História da Universidade Presbiteriana Mackenzie. Pedagoga pela Pontifícia Universidade Católica de São Paulo (PUC-SP).

PhD in Social History from the Faculty of Philosophy, Liberal Arts and Human Sciences, University of São Paulo (FFLCH-USP). Master in School Psychology and Human Development (IP-USP). Professor of the Graduate Program in Education, Art and History of Culture and of the History Course of the Mackenzie Presbyterian University. Pedagogue by the Pontifical Catholic University of São Paulo (PUC-SP).

Irene Patrícia Nohara

Livre-Docente e Doutora em Direito do Estado pela Faculdade de Direito da USP. Professora-Pesquisadora do Programa de Direito Político e Econômico da Universidade Presbiteriana Mackenzie (UPM).

Full-Professor and PhD. in State Law from University of São Paulo (USP). Professor-Researcher from the Political and Economic Law Program at the Mackenzie Presbyterian University.

João Clemente de S. Neto

Possui mestrado e doutorado em Ciências Sociais, e pós-doutorado em Sociologia Clínica, pela Pontifícia Universidade Católica de São Paulo. É professor adjunto, pesquisador e orientador no Programa de Pós-Graduação em Educação, Arte e História da Cultura e no Curso de Graduação em Pedagogia da Universidade Presbiteriana Mackenzie.

He holds a master's and doctorate in Social Sciences and a post-doctorate in Clinical Sociology from the Pontifical Catholic University of São Paulo. He is an adjunct professor, researcher, and advisor in the Postgraduate Program in Education, Art, and History of Culture and the Undergraduate Course in Pedagogy at Mackenzie Presbyterian University.

Jörg Schröder

Professor da Cátedra de Design Territorial e Planejamento Urbano da Leibniz Universität Hannover (LUH). Pró-Reitor de Pesquisa da Faculdade de Arquitetura e Ciências Paisagistas. Arquiteto e Urbanista.

Professor of the Chair of Territorial Design and Urban Planning at Leibniz Universität Hannover (LUH). Dean for Research of the Faculty of Architecture and Landscape Sciences. Architect and Urban Planner.

Julia Motte-Baumvol
Pós-doutorado em Direito pela Universidade de Genebra e Doutora em Direito pela Universidade Paris I – Panthéon-Sorbonne. Professora de Direito Publico na Universidade Paris Cité.
Pos-doctor in Law from Geneve University and PhD in Law from the University Paris I – Panthéon-Sorbonne. Professor of Public Law at Université Paris City.

Luca Rossato
Doutor em Arquitetura e Planejamento Urbano, Mestre em Planejamento Urbano e Regional nos Países em Desenvolvimento, Professor Assistente RTDb (ICAR 17) no Departamento de Arquitetura, Universidade de Ferrara (Itália). Arquiteto.
PhD in Architecture and Urban Planning, Master in Urban and Regional Planning in Developing Countries and, Assistant Professor RTDb (ICAR /17) at the Department of Architecture, University of Ferrara (Italy). Architect.

Matteo Finco
Pesquisador de Pós-Graduação no Departamento de Ciências Sociais e Econômicas da Università degli Studi di Roma "La Sapienza" e Pesquisador Colaborador no Centre for Socio-Economic Research on Ageing of IRCCS-INRCA (National Institute of Health and Science on Ageing) em Ancona, Itália.
Post-doctoral researcher at the Department of Social Sciences and Economics of Università degli Studi di Roma "La Sapienza" and collaborating researcher at the Centre for Socio-Economic Research on Ageing of IRCCS-INRCA (National Institute of Health and Science on Ageing) in Ancona (Italy).

Natalia Feld
Doutoranda em Estudos Urbanos na Universidade Nacional de General Sarmiento (Buenos Aires). Mestre em Economia Urbana pela Universidad Torcuato Di Tella. Professora e pesquisadora do Instituto del Conurbano (ICO) na Universidad Nacional de General Sarmiento (UNGS). Arquiteta (Universidade de Buenos Aires).

PhD student in Urban Studies at the National University of General Sarmiento (Buenos Aires). Master in Urban Economics from Universidad Torcuato Di Tella. Professor and researcher at Instituto del Conurbano (ICO) of the the National University of General Sarmiento (UNGS). Architect.

Orlando Villas Bôas Filho

Possui graduação em História na Universidade de São Paulo, em Direito na Pontifícia Universidade Católica de São Paulo e em Filosofia na Universidade de São Paulo. É mestre e doutor em Direito pela Universidade de São Paulo. Realizou Pós-Doutorado na Université de Paris X – Nanterre e na École Normale Supérieure de Paris. Recebeu o Prêmio Capes de Teses em 2007 (concedido à melhor tese defendida no Brasil, em 2006, na área do Direito). Atualmente, é Professor da Faculdade de Direito da Universidade de São Paulo (FD/USP) e da Faculdade de Direito da Universidade Presbiteriana Mackenzie.
Graduated in History at the University of São Paulo, in Law at the Pontifical Catholic University of São Paulo and in Philosophy at the University of São Paulo. He holds master's and doctorate degrees in law from the University of São Paulo. He did Postdoctoral research at the Université de Paris X-Nanterre and at the École Normale Supérieure de Paris. He received the Capes de Teses Award in 2007 (granted to the best thesis defended in Brazil, in 2006, in the area of Law). Currently, he is Professor at the Faculty of Law of the University of São Paulo (USP) and at the Faculty of Law of the Presbyterian Mackenzie University Law School (UPM).

Rosana M. P.B. Schwartz

Doutora em História pela PUC-SP. Mestre em Educação, Arte e História da Cultura. Especialista em Artes pelo Instituto Teresa Gerini – Roma/Itália. Professora da Universidade Presbiteriana Mackenzie – Pós Graduação – Mestrado e Doutorado em Educação, Arte e História da Cultura. Disciplinas – Cultura e Pensamento Social, Metodologia da Pesquisa em História da Cultura, Brasil: uma breve história cultural. Na Graduação – Curso de Pedagogia. Professora da Pontifícia Universidade Católica – PUC-SP – COGEAe – Pós-Graduação Lato Senso – História, Sociedade e Cultura. Líder do grupo de Pesquisa – História da Cultura, Sociedades e Mídias – Mackenzie. Integrante do Núcleo de Pesquisa sobre a Mulher da PUC-SP. Pesquisadora Ad hoc da Secretaria Especial de Políticas para as Mulheres.

PhD in History from PUC-SP. Master in Education, Art and Cultural History. Specialist in Arts at the Teresa Gerini Institute – Rome/Italy. Professor at Mackenzie Presbyterian University – Postgraduate – Masters and Doctorate in Education, Art and History of Culture. Subjects – Culture and Social Thought, Research Methodology in Cultural History, Brazil: a brief cultural history. Undergraduate – Pedagogy course. Professor at the Pontifical Catholic University / PUC / SP – COGEAe – Postgraduate Lato Senso – History, Society and Culture. Leader of the Research Group – History of Culture, Societies and Media – Mackenzie. Member of the Women's Research Center at PUC-SP. Ad hoc researcher for the Special Secretariat for Women's Policies.

Solange Teles da Silva

Pós-doutorado em Direito pela Universidade Paris I – Panthéon-Sorbonne. Professora da Faculdade de Direito, Universidade Presbiteriana Mackenzie – São Paulo. Bolsista Produtividade em pesquisa CNPq. Lider do Grupo de Pesquisa CNPq Direito e Desenvolvimento Sustentável. Membro do Projeto de Pesquisa CAPES/PRINT Cidade, Projeto e Equidade: das Linguagens e Apropriações às formas de Regulação.

Pos-Doctor and PhD in Law from the University Paris I – Panthéon-Sorbonne. Professor at the Faculty of Law, Presbyterian Mackenzie University – São Paulo. CNPq Research Productivity Scholarship. Leader of the CNPq Research Group on Law and Sustainable Development. CAPES Print/UPM Project The social scale: language, cities and culture – Project «City, Project and Equity: from languages and appropriations to forms of regulation.

Tarin Cristino Frota Mont'Alverne

Doutora em Direito Internacional do Meio Ambiente pela Universidade de Paris V e pela Universidade de São Paulo. Professora da Faculdade de Direito da Universidade Federal do Ceara. Bolsista Produtividade em Pesquisa CNPq. Coordenadora do Grupo de Estudos em Direito e Relações Internacionais (GEDAI).

PhD in International Environmental Law from the University of Paris V and University of São Paulo. Professor at the Faculty of Law of the Federal University of Ceará. CNPq Research Productivity Scholarship. Coordinator of the Study Group in Law and International Affairs (GEDAI).

PREFACE

In times of fear, closed doors, railings and the construction of walls, professors Wilson Florio and Fabio Ramazzini Bechara dare to address the theme 'City, Project and Equity: from Languages and Appropriations to Forms of Regulation', organizing chapters of ideas, proposals and hope of several colleagues, who, like them and us, believe in the city as a collective space.

Thus, those who are enchanted by the shapes of the buildings, or the old houses famous for their stories scattered around the city, or even with the living art, painted on the walls of tall buildings or on the walls of the city, will be able to find in this work, themes that no deal with art and culture; the means of expression and artistic and/or architectural representation, languages guided by technologies, projects and works of buildings and the forms of urban regulation mediated by the norm and legislation.

However as space is not founded only on art and beauty, we can also find chapters that deal with historical and environmental heritage, sustainable and equitable development of Brazilian cities, intervention and regulation of urban space and the production and socio-spatial production of the formal and informal city. An example of this is the current discussions about smart cities maximizing changes, with minimal costs or even with the participation of locals (in Street Lighting, Security, for example).

Finally, there is the issue that has been increasingly urgent and more expensive for everyone who uses public space and who faces social problems such as poverty, lack of housing, sanitation, resulting in the occupation of the city by the people who live in poverty, who build their houses under overpasses, squares and close to subway stations, and who, without an inclusion project, are marginalized at the edge of park gates, which were formerly squares.

Therefore, the work also addresses the improvement in the use of spaces, in a thoughtful and organized way, considering the equity and inequality of urban living conditions, the challenges to coexistence in society, characterized by mobility, increased diversity and intolerance, new forms of housing, identity and alterity.

The themes were thought from the appropriation of spaces by all who live there and it is in this sense that when we deal with the theme of urbanism, the need we have to perceive the other comes to mind. And this is alterity.

This is the mission of the present work, organized by the brilliant colleagues Wilson Florio and Fábio Bechara who, specialists in the subject who seek to deepen the theme to present different realities and thus, look at common problems, from the perspective of the other, thinking together possible legal solutions that always address inclusion, popular participation in this movement and the exercise of citizenship that requires alterity from all of us.

FELIPE CHIARELLO DE SOUZA PINTO

SUMARY

INTRODUCTION

Globalization can be defined as the enhancement of social relationships on a world scale which impose unequal growth. The change of paradigm caused by the conversion of national societies into globalized societies results in severe challenges in dealing with social and environmental issues. The increasing unbalance between freedom and individual rights weaken human ties. Thus, in this time of crisis, existential uncertainty is rooted on the fragility and volatility of social ties.

Debates on environmental issues, global, sustainable, and smart cities, on social media and gender issues, among others, which took place in the last decade, spring from the wide changes caused by globalization and world modernity. As the state fades in the face of new global powers, insecurity, inequality, and instability in work relationships increase and are compounded by serious environmental, housing, and social problems. By progressively abandoning or renouncing its responsibilities and roles as a provider of certainty, security, and rights for its citizens, the State creates great misfortunes in urban life and contributes to the neglect of public spaces, thus generating a feeling of uncertainty which leads to a lack of professional perspective and commitment to the collective (the entire urban community).

The rapid verticalization and densification of large cities bring up great challenges to be tackled, such as in human mobility, the preservation of cultural heritage, the quality of public spaces, laws and guidelines, urban infrastructure, the coexistence between citizens, and the quality of life. Social relationships, the appreciation of culture, and fast urban changes brought about by a globalized world require actions that, while safeguarding major values, do not hinder development and necessary growth in a time of accelerated change. In the digital era, continuous flow, instantaneous exchanges of information, and deterritorialization make space irrelevant, mainly public spaces where people spend time together. Thus, it is essential to understand the current process of human mobility.

The degradation of public spaces is a visible fact that complicates the establishment of quality places to stay. Gated communities are answers to the crisis of public spaces. People's isolation in private spaces is a sign of fear in the face of the unexpected that may be found in public space. The precariousness of central areas in large cities shows the tough reality of the frailty of human relationships: inequalities, neglect, violence, and intolerance. Governments which had once been the guardians of the laws that assured collective welfare are now powerless in the face of urban degradation and violence. In addition, public policies aimed at deregulation, flexibility, and privatization increasingly aggravate this process.

As a consequence, the striking inability to deal with differences, characterized by intolerance in accepting contrasting views, evinces a breach with collective and universal values. Everything indicates that the quest for universal rights and respect for differences should be the focus of our future concerns.

The outbreak of globalization in the early 1990s brought along the internationalization not only of commerce, but also of education and inter-institutional research. Likewise, it is one of the results of the changes in the notion of space-time, in which a surge of interchange, visiting-professor, post-doctoral programs etc. attempts to connect institutions and individuals in research networks. In this sense, the projects and researches mentioned here have also contributed to this debate.

The current need to interpret facts from an interdisciplinary point of view comes from the fragmentation and specialization of knowledge, in which each researcher analyses only his own discipline with a very specific focus, thus losing sight of the whole in which his research and teaching activity is inserted. Therefore, current complex problems cannot be treated by professionals from a single field of knowledge.

To handle this complexity, we have to create a pool of professionals to act together and work not only in interdisciplinary, but also in trans-disciplinary ways. Sciences develop precisely through information and knowledge exchange and by means of interaction. Consequently, it is clear that adopting a practice that integrates knowledge, exchange and interdisciplinary experiences, favours the perception and construction of collective knowledge.

This book is, therefore, a result of developing networked research and international exchanges enabled by CAPES' Institutional Internationalization Program (PrInt). It is impossible not to recognize in this praiseworthy scientific program an opportunity to build new academic and human links, which entail a qualitative improvement in the level of our technical production.

If PrInt has allowed us to reap good results, this is also due to the efforts of professors, executive technicians and students from the Graduate Programs in Political and Economic Law (PPGDPE) and in Architecture and Urbanism (PPGAU). We have combined our skills, complemented our points of view and consolidated investigations of great practical and intellectual value to establish links between fields of research and activity. This work, which was born from this alliance, presents articles produced in co-authorship by professors and students of Mackenzie Presbyterian University in São Paulo, as well as by faculty members associated with important training and research centres in other countries.

We have a natural tendency to favour our own position, that is, we are inclined to defend our own point of view (MOLDEN; HIGGINS, 2005), which can lead to poor conclusions when making decisions. We often draw conclusions and inferences based on little evidence (RITCHARD; PERKINS, 2005; PERKINS, 1995). The interaction and exchange of experiences between professionals from different fields of knowledge forces us to change this situation in order to perceive a whole new spectrum of possibilities for interpreting and evaluating the same facts.

Building facts is a collective process. Each researcher adds a layer onto previous knowledge so as to decrease disagreements and advance towards truth, even though we admit that truth is always provisional in the field of science.

Sciences are not autonomous, because they depend on collective actions. Academic investigations are not carried out only within universities, neither are they restricted to knowledge produced in laboratories. Several strands should be addressed by researchers who wish to carry out an investigation which has a greater impact on their performance field.

A systems view, favoured by interdisciplinarity, enhances this kind of knowledge construction and exchange. Complexity contains a multiplicity in which the whole is much bigger than the sum of its parts. Facing complexity implies facing uncertainty and doubt as starting points to generate reflection and self-knowledge.

In the article "Costal Cities and Climate Change in Brazil: Challenges and Perspectives", professors Solange Teles da Silva, Julia Motte-Baumvol, and Tarin Cristino Frota Mont'Alverne address the combination of factors involved in climatic change in coastal cities, showing a sensitive relationship between human interactions in urban spaces and the climate changes that result from these interventions. Since coastal cities are densely populated spaces, identifying the direct relationship between humans and the climate requires, in the authors' view, a regulatory arrangement that may ensure development in conjunction with climate justice, since climate is one of the essential factors for human development.

In the chapter titled "Eladio Dieste's Inventive Design and Building – The Discontinuous Gaussian Vaults", professors Felipe Corres Melachos, Wilson Florio, Federica Maietti, and Luca Rossato analyse the Uruguayan engineer's innovative work in designing curved roofs. From the drawings produced by the engineer, it was possible to identify a regular defining geometry in the undulating surfaces that overcome large spans. Parametric modelling has contributed to identify the "algebraic" formula underlying geometry, demonstrating the permanence of a constructive thought that made construction possible.

Professors Orlando Villas Bôas Filho and Matteo Finco present the article "Urban Space, Social Exclusion and 'Legality Regimes': An Approach Based on Étienne Le Roy's 'Theory of Multilegalism'", in which they discuss the reflections of urban and social exclusion in official and unofficial regulatory dynamics, many of which appear as life-management mechanisms for socially marginalized groups, doing without the state as a source of normativity. From Étienne Le Roy's notion of multilegalism, the authors present an innovative analytical perspective to include environments marked by hybrid and multiple social relationships, as occurs in spaces of social exclusion.

In the chapter "Corridors and Arches: Portraits of a Dichotomy Within Dematerialising Networks", professors Laura Abbruzzese, Valter Caldana, and Romeo Farinella reflect on the different meanings of the concept of "corridor", ranging from a space within a building to a whole territory. On the other hand, the idea of "arch" is analysed from the primordial geometrically-defined constructive element to its understanding as a symbol for defining places, networks, and an urban territory.

From their research on expressions involving graffiti, professors Irene Nohara, Carlos Leite, and Elisabete Castanheira have analysed the plurality of perceptions and uses of urban space as well as how regulation has kept up with the dynamic of those expressions, choosing the city of São Paulo as their analytical field. In "Creative and Social Innovative Potentialities in São Paulo: The Case of Graffiti and the Regulated Transformation of Urban Space", the authors address an agenda for the city based on the notion of the socio-political regulation of transforming urban spaces by means of art and culture, counting on the leadership of public agents and on a regulatory perspective that makes this proposal for artistic intervention in the city feasible.

Professors Ingrid Ambrogi, Rosana Schwartz, and João Clemente Neto, along with Axel Föller-Mancini and Bernhard Johannes Fichtner, wrote the chapter called "University Projects and Human Mobility: Contemporary Perspectives for a City that Can Educate and Accommodate". They address topics regarding the connection between individuals and their territories, highlighting the construction of identity which results from their integration (or lack of it) into the places they inhabit. Educational spaces, artistic interventions, and public spaces are studied in order to identify actions that promote better social and educational coexistence.

Fernando de Oliveira Domingues Ladeira, a student from the Graduate Program in Political and Economic Law in our university, presents the article "Translating City Walls: Space and Symbolic Power", in which the relationship between the city and its human inhabitants is mediated by a symbolic relationship that impacts directly on subjects' individuality, mainly regarding the nature of their relationship with urban space. Therefore, cities as symbolic horizons are the author's central topic as he follows a path that allows him to envisage the importance of making urban space more and more accessible to different publics so that they may build themselves together with the city.

In the chapter *Dynamics of periphery in Sao Paulo: reflections on possible pathways progressing towards social resilience*, professors Carlos Leite and Angélica Benatti Alvim, professor Jörg Schröder, from Leibniz Universität

Hannover, and two young PhDs Andresa Ledo Marques and Daniela Getlinger, reflect on the trajectory of the changes in the poor, outlying neighbourhoods of the city of São Paulo in the context of the need to overcome the metropolis' fragmentation. Recent experiences point to new perspectives in order to develop innovative forms of integrating urban plans in vulnerable territories.

Lastly, in the chapter "Proyecto urbanos versus operaciones inmobiliarias: acerca del Dique 1 en Puerto Madero, Buenos Aires", researchers Alicia Novick, Eunice Helena Abascal, Natalia Feld, and Angélica Benatti Alvim investigate the process of renovation of the buildings in Puerto Madero, Buenos Aires, looking at the normative instruments of urban planning. The authors highlight the conditions of implementation and the procedures resulting from the direction established by the Master Plan designed to rehabilitate the urban intervention area. In addition to the subordination of the state to private companies, the research reveals that it was possible to show that Dyke 1 ceased to be an element of urban design and became a set of real estate developments unrelated to the original idea.

We wish you all an excellent study!

The organizers.

FABIO RAMAZZINI BECHARA
FELIPE CHIARELLO DE SOUZA PINTO
WILSON FLORIO

1. COASTAL CITIES AND CLIMATE CHANGE IN BRAZIL, CHALLENGES AND PERSPECTIVES[1]

Solange Teles da Silva
Julia Motte-Baumvol
Tarin Cristino Frota Mont'Alverne

Introduction

The relationships between climate change and coastal cities involve different spatial scales and thus different scales of regulation in the way in which spaces and natural resources are used and appropriated. Such relationships include an analysis of the effects of extreme weather phenomena, which result among other consequences, changes in the volume of precipitation, floods, droughts and heat waves, as well as an increase in sea level. But there is also another aspect to climate change in addition to the technical issues, the collapse of infrastructure and loss of access to essential services: the human aspect. In fact, « [p]oor people are disproportionately affected by climate impacts, which could push an additional 100 million people into extreme poverty by 2030»[2].

[1] This article is the result of the CAPES Print/UPM Project mission. The social scale: language, cities and culture – Project «City, Project and Equity: from languages and appropriations to forms of regulation» taken place in October 2021 – University of Paris Descartes, France and the consolidation of the UPM/Université Paris Descartes/UFC research network.

[2] BOYD, David R. UN Human Rights Council Special Rapporteur on the Issue of Human Rights Obligations Relating to the Enjoyment of a Safe, Clean, Healthy and Sustainable Environment (A/74/161), New York, 15 July 2019, p. 5. Available at: < https://digitallibrary.un.org/record/3814570> Access 20 Dec. 2021.

And it is precisely this human aspect of climate change, which little by little has gained expression and visibility, that is emphasized in this essay from the perspective of vulnerabilities, justice and equity in coastal cities. This is because it is precisely in coastal cities that a large part of the human population is found and that is where these issues are exacerbated and call attention to the "climate emergency"[3] and the possibilities that bring the norms that lead a "climatization" of public policies.

Therefore, the objective of this essay is to carry out a reflection, based on the plurality of normative spaces, on the construction of legal strategies for mitigating and adapting the effects of climate change in coastal cities and, in particular in Brazilian coastal cities, under the prism of vulnerabilities, justice and equity. Consequently, based on a reflection on the relationship between cities and climate change, we dive into the analysis of this essay, focusing on Brazilian coastal cities with their vulnerabilities. We then look at the relationship between climate change, human rights and coastal cities, highlighting the challenges to be considered in the climate justice context. As complement to this discussion, we work with the perspective of the intrinsic relationship between biodiversity and climate change in coastal cities, which brings to the discussion the concept of Nature-Based Solutions (NBS) and the perspectives of its diffusion in coastal areas to face the effects of climate change.

1. Coastal cities and climate change

Brazil has a coastline of more than 8,500 km in lengh[4], in which 17 member states and 300 coastal municipalities[5] are bathed by the Atlantic

[3] In fact, in terms of scientific evidence of the climate emergency, the First IPCC report already indicated the profound changes that climate change could cause in human societies and ecosystems. HOUGHTON, John Theodore; JENKINS, G.J.; EPHRAUMS J.J.,(eds). Climate Change: The IPCC Scientific Assessment, 1990. Group I. IPCC, Cambridge, UK: Cambridge Univ. Press, 1993. As Christel Cournil underlines, «the climate emergency no longer needs to be demonstrated and since the last three years it has been increasingly 'proclaimed' by certain States, regions, metropolises, cities, as a priority field of public action. » (Free translation) COURNIL, Christel. Introduction. In COURNIL, Christel (right) La fabrique d'un droit climatique: au service de la route '1.5'. Paris: Pedone, 2021, p. 17.

[4] Considering cuts and reentries.

[5] MARENGO, José A.; SCARANO, Fabio R. (eds.) Impacto, vulnerabilidade e adaptação das cidades costeiras brasileiras às mudanças climáticas. Relatório Especial do Painel Brasileiro de Mudanças Climáticas. PBMC, COPPE – UFRJ, 2016, p. 15. Disponível em <https://

Ocean. Among the «42 Brazilian metropolitan regions, 18 are located in the coastal area or are influenced by it»[6]. If, on one hand, 40% of the world population lives in coastal areas[7], in Brazil more than 60% of the Brazilian population lives in such areas.[8] Exposed to the rising number of extreme rainfall events, both in terms of frequency and intensity, which elevates the risk of landslides, floods and flash floods, as well as coastal erosion and sea level rise, Brazilian coastal cities and their respective human populations must then prepare to face the risks associated with climate change.

According to the Intergovernmental Oceanographic Commission (IOC) linked to UNESCO, these risks related to climate change in coastal areas can be classified as rapid-onset risks such as tsunami, sea level rise and waves generated by extreme winds or even cumulative or progressive risks such as sea level rise and coastal erosion.[9] But environmental risks

ppgoceano.paginas.ufsc.br/files/2017/06/Relatorio_DOIS_v1_04.06.17.pdf> Access 20 Dec. 2021. In addition to the 280 Municipalities facing the sea, defined in a list established by the IBGE, there are also municipalities that are not facing the sea, but that are included in the terrestrial band of the coastal zone because they (i) are in coastal metropolitan regions, (ii) are contiguous with the capitals and large coastal cities that present conurbation, (iii) are distant up to fifty kilometers from the coastline, which include, in their territory, activities or infrastructure of great environmental impact in the coastal zone or coastal ecosystems of high relevance (art. 4th). of Decree 5,300/2004). IBGE. Municípios defrontantes com o mar 2020. IBGE. Municípios defrontantes com o mar 2020. Disponível em: < https://geoftp.ibge.gov.br/organizacao_do_territorio/estrutura_territorial/municipios_defrontantes_com_o_mar/2020/Municipios_Defrontantes_com_o_Mar_2020.pdf> Acesso em 22.10.2021. BRASIL. Decreto n. 5.300, de 7 de dezembro de 2004, que regulamenta a Lei n. 7.661, de 16 de maio de 1988, que institui o Plano Nacional de Gerenciamento Costeiro – PNGC, dispõe sobre regras de uso e ocupação da zona costeira e estabelece critérios de gestão da orla marítima, e dá outras providências.

[6] MARENGO, José A.; SCARANO, Fabio R. (eds.) *Op. cit.*, p. 13.

[7] UNFCCC. Policy Brief Technologies for Averting, Minimizing and Addressing Loss and Damage in Coastal Zone. Executive Committee of the Warsaw International Mechanism for Loss and Damage – Technology Executive Committee, 2020. Available at: https://unfccc.int/ttclear/misc_/StaticFiles/gnwoerk_static/2020_coastalzones/cfecc85aaa8d43d38cd0f6ceae2b61e4/2bb696550804403fa08df8a924922c2e.pdf Access 20 Dec. 2021.

[8] *Idem, ibidem.*

[9] IOC – Intergovernmental Oceanographic Commission. *Hazard awareness and risk mitigation in integrated coastal area management. United Nations Educational, Scientific and Cultural Organization (UNESCO)*, Manuals and Guides No 50, ICAM Dossier No 5, 141p., Paris, França, 2009. Available at: <http://legacy.ioc-unesco.org/index.php?option=com_oe&task=viewDocumentRecord&docID=3947> Access 20 Dec. 2021.

can also be considered, as Nicoladi and Petermann point out, based on the result of three categories: (i) natural risk associated to processes and events of natural origin or induced by human activities»[10], (ii) technological risk, resulting from production processes, (iii) social risk, « resulting from social needs for full human development that contribute to the degradation of living conditions ».[11] The authors then, by examine these three risks, define five levels of vulnerability and identify the scenario that emerges and brings the challenges for the country's integrated coastal management facing climate change.[12]

The Special Report of the Brazilian Panel on Climate Change: Impact, vulnerability and adaptation of Brazilian coastal cities to climate change in 2016 brings the state-of-the-art knowledge of the impacts of the effects of climate change in these cities, showing that

> « Coastal cities are particularly vulnerable to the impacts of climate change and its consequences, such as rising sea levels, heat waves, floods and droughts. In the case of Brazilian coastal cities, deficiencies in urban infrastructure and concentration of poor residents at risk accentuate this vulnerability. »[13].

The concept of vulnerability is not univocal. In fact, different interpretations of the meanings can be associated with the term vulnerability, whether from the biophysical aspects, considering the individuals or social groups most vulnerable to climate change, such as indigenous and non-indigenous traditional communities – *quilombolas*[14], fishermen

[10] NICOLADI, Joao Luiz; PETERMANN, Rafael Mueller. Mudanças climáticas e a Vulnerabilidade da Zona Costeira do Brasil: Aspectos ambientais, sociais e tecnológicos. In *Revista de Gestão Costeira*, 10(2), 2010, p. 153. Available at: < https://www.aprh.pt/rgci/pdf/rgci-206_Nicolodi.pdf> Access 20 Dec. 2021.

[11] *Idem, ibidem.*

[12] *Idem, ibidem.*

[13] MARENGO, Jose A.; SCARANO, Fabio R. *Op. cit.*, p. 129.

[14] «The quilombola communities are social groups whose ethnic identity distinguishes them from the rest of society. According to the definition of the Associação Brasileira de Antropologia (Brazilian Anthropology Association), quilombola communities 'are groups who developed resistance practices in the maintenance and reproduction of their characteristic ways of life in a determined place.' The origin of such groups is related to the process of resistance to slavery, which subjugated blacks brought from Africa to Brazil for 300 years.

and fisherwomen, shellfish gatherers, among others – or by carrying out an analysis based on the multiple factors and processes that influence both individual vulnerability and their ability to respond to the effects of climate change[15]. There is this difference in these interpretations though they are complementary.

The term «vulnerability» was expressly adopted in the United Nations Framework Convention on Climate Change (UNFCCC) referring to the need of assistance of those «vulnerability» States

> The specific needs and special circumstances of developing country Parties, especially those that are particularly vulnerable to the adverse effects of climate change, and of those Parties, especially developing country Parties, that would have to bear a disproportionate or abnormal burden under the Convention, should be given full consideration (art. 3.2. UNFCCC)

Thus the convention addresses the vulnerability of developing states.[16] Climate change «will exacerbate existing poverty and inequality»[17] in States with devastating effects on coastal cities.

The quilombola communities were formed from a wide variety of processes, both during the slavery regime and after the abolition of slavery in the 19th century, facing inequalities that are perpetuated through to the present day. Their identity is defined by 'the experience and shared vision of their common past as well as their continuity as a group. Therefore, the quilombolas have a common historical reference constructed from shared experiences and values'. Quilombola communities are characterized by the common use of their territories, conceived by them as a collective and indivisible space occupied and utilized through consensual rules respected by the various family groups that make up the communities and based on solidarity and mutual assistance». COMMUNIQUÉ REGARDING THE FULFILLMENT BY THE BRAZILIAN GOVERNMENT OF ILO CONVENTION 169 ADDRESSING INDIGENOUS AND TRIBAL PEOPLES, 2018. Available at: < https://cpisp.org.br/wp-content/uploads/2018/09/CommuniqueRegardingtheFulfillmentBytheBrazilian GovernmentofiloConvention169AddressingIndigenousandTribalPeoples_2008.pdf> Access 20 Dec. 2021.

15 IWAMA, Allan Yu et al. Risk, Vulnerability and Adaptation to Climate Change: an Interdisciplinary Approach. In Ambie. Soc. 19 (2), Apr-Jun 2016. Available at: < https://doi.org/10.1590/1809 -4422ASOC137409V1922016> Access 20 Dec. 2021.

16 MBOYA, Atieno. Vulnerability and the Climate Change Regime. In *UCLA Journal of Environmental Law and Policy*, 36 (1), 2018, pp. 79-103.

17 HUMANS RIGHTS COUNCIL. Climate change and poverty – Report of the Special Rapporteur on extreme poverty and human rights (A/HRC/41/39), 17 July 2019, p. 4. Available at: < https://undocs.org/en/A/HRC/41/39> Access 20 Dec. 2021.

> «Coastal countries face high risks from the impacts of projected climate change; in coastal zones such risks are exacerbated by additional factors, such as compound floods and coastal land subsidence. The concentration of people, assets and socioeconomic activities in coastal zones make them particularly vulnerable and in urgent need of proactive protective action. Climate impacts along with population increases will further exacerbate the expected damage to infrastructure and the vulnerability of coastal populations. SROCC emphasizes the importance of climate-geared adaptation of coastal zones and that adaptation measures generate many co-benefits at different scales». [18]

On the one hand, individuals and social groups will be more affected because they often live in areas more exposed to the risks of climate change, in precarious housing and having fewer resources to adapt to the effects of climate change. On the other hand, developing countries will have to bear between about 75 to 80% of the costs[19] of climate change and among these countries Brazil. Thus, the climate emergency demands actions at different regulatory scales, considering issues of equity and climate justice.

2. Climate change and human rights in coastal cities

The relationship between climate change and human rights can be observed either through: (i) the understanding that a right to an ecologically balanced environment presupposes appropriate measures in relation to the climate or (ii) the insertion of human rights in the climate regime. Literature also has an important role in the discussions and more profound look at this theme,[20] indicating clues for reflection on this issue

[18] UNFCCC. Policy Brief Technologies for Averting, Minimizing and Addressing Loss and Damage in Coastal Zone. Executive Committee of the Warsaw International Mechanism for Loss and Damage – Technology Executive Committee, 2020, p. 16. Available at: < https://unfccc.int/ttclear/misc_/StaticFiles/gnwoerk_static/2020_coastalzones/b9e88f6fea374d8aa5cb44115d201160/3863c9fabdf74ea49710189acbf6907a.pdf> Access 20 Dec. 2021.

[19] *Idem, ibidem.*

[20] BODANSKY, Daniel. Introduction: climate change and human rights: unpacking the issues. In *Georgia Journal of International and Comparative Law* vol. 38, n. 3, 2010, pp. 511-524. McLNERNEY-LANKFORD, Siobhán, DARROW, Mac, RAJAMANI, Lavanya. Human rights and climate change: a review of the international legal dimensions. Washington: World Bank, 2011.

from the climate justice concept.[21] The principles of equity and common but differentiated responsibilities[22], enshrined by UNFCCC and in the Paris Agreement[23], materialize the implementation of this concept internationally, but it must also be understood that climate justice can be analyzed domestically of each country and between different social groups. As Leroy states, climate justice can be understood as:

> «a set of principles that ensures that no group of people, be their ethnic, racial or class groups, supports a disproportionate amount of degradation of the collective space caused by climate change, which seriously compromises the quality of life and makes its reproduction and the forces you to migrate»[24].

Based on this, how can we ensure that no group of people in coastal areas, indigenous and traditional peoples, such as artisanal fishermen and fisherwomen, shellfish gatherers, "caiçaras", black women and men, and other vulnerable groups do not bear a disproportionate share of the negative effects of climate change? How can the relationship between human rights and climate change provide answers and ensure the rights of a vulnerable portion of the population residing in the coastal area?

From the human rights point of view,[25] according to David R. Boyd report, Special Rapporteur on human rights obligations related to benefit with a safe, clean, healthy and sustainable means, recommended to the United Nations General Assembly in July 2019, *«The poorest half of the world's population, 3.9 billion people, generate only 10 percent of global emissions.*

[21] SILVA, Solange Teles da; RAMOS, Marina C.. Justiça climática: desafios e perspectivas a partir de uma análise das decisões dos Tribunais Superiores Brasileiros. In: AYALA, Patryck. (Org.). *O Direito das mudanças climáticas: normatividade e princípios para a justiça ecológica no direito nacional e internacional.* 1ed.Curitiba: CRV, 2020, v. 1, p. 77-96.

[22] Art. 3. UNFCCC.

[23] Art. 2.2 Paris Agreement.

[24] LEROY, Jean Pierre. 2009. Justiça climática: um direito humano negado. In *Democracia Viva* n. 43, 2009, p. 3-4.

[25] It is important to highlight the work of the rapporteur John Knox who presented in 2018 the perspective of the «greening» of human rights. UNGA. Human rights obligations relating to the enjoyment of a safe, clean, healthy and sustainable environment – Report of the Special Rapporteur John H. Knox, (A/73/188), 19 July 2018. Available at: <https://undocs. org/en/A/73/188 > Access 20 Dec. 2021.

Conversely, the richest 10 percent produce half of global emissions»[26]. And, those who have contributed the least to climate change disproportionately suffer its effects without having sufficient means to protect themselves or adapt. In terms of national states, Brazil among the 20 countries that contribute with ¾ of the world's greenhouse gas emissions, as pointed out by data from the *Global Carbon Atlas*[27] – 2021, notably due to deforestation, which intensified 2018 onwards, pushed by agriculture and particularly by livestock.[28]

And climate change has considerable repercussions on various human rights as Boyd points out, such as «*the right to life, health, food, water and sanitation, to a healthy environment, to a sufficient standard of living, housing, property, self-determination, development and culture*»[29], with State obligations to protect human rights in view of environmental damage and international commitments assumed by States.

The Paris Agreement adopted in December 2015 and put into effect November 2016 clearly recognized the importance of human rights in its preamble and invited States to respect and promote their human rights obligations when taking action to combat climate change.[30] And this to achieve its three objectives, which are: (i) to contain the rise in the average temperature of the planet below 2ºC in relation to pre-industrial levels and to continue the action to limit the rise in temperature to 1ºC, (ii) to reinforce adapting capacities in the face of the harmful effects of climate change, (iii) making financial flows compatible with the profile of evolution towards a development with low emissions of greenhouse gases and resilient to climate change. However, if such objectives must be based on measures that respect human rights, the Katowice climate package, the

[26] BOYD, David R. *op. cit.*, p. 7.

[27] Global Carbon Project. *Global Carbon Atlas 2021*. Available at: http://www.globalcarbonatlas.org/en/content/welcome-carbon-atlas Access 20 Dec. 2021.

[28] BERENGUER, Erika et. al. Drivers and Ecological Impacts of Deforestation and Forest Degradation. In SCIENCE PANEL FOR THE AMAZON. Amazon Assessment Report 2021. Available at: https://www.theamazonwewant.org/amazon-assessment-report-2021/ Access 20 Dec. 2021.

[29] *Idem*, p. 11.

[30] It is certain that in 2010 the Cancun Agreement made reference for the first time towards human rights. UNFCCC. Decision 1/CP. 16 The Cancun Agreements: Outcome of the work of the Ad Hoc Working Group on Long-term Cooperative Action under the Convention.

complex package of rules designed to guide the implementation of this agreement, omit this issue regarding human rights. Now, discussions on human rights play an important role in indicating parameters for climate action and protecting the most vulnerable ones, in order to correct the current disparities that exclude the poor from building strategies for the climate emergency. Thus, according to Boyd, to comply with human rights obligations «States should apply a rights-based approach to all aspects of climate change and climate action»,[31] considering three categories of state obligations[32]:

(i) procedural, such as access to information in an accessible and understandable way, access to the potential impacts of climate change and human rights in public plans and policies, respect for indigenous rights and in particular free, prior and informed consent;
(ii) substantial, which imposes on the «States must not violate the right to a safe climate through their own actions»[33], avoiding discrimination and measures that may indicate a regression of rights, and
(iii) specific obligations regarding vulnerable situations. Regarding these last obligations, it can be observed that:

> «States should take effective measures to raise the awareness of environmental threats among those persons who are most at risk. In monitoring and reporting on environmental issues, States should provide detailed information on the threats to, and status of, the most vulnerable. Assessments of the environmental and human rights impacts of proposed projects and policies must include a careful examination of the impacts on the most vulnerable, in particular. In the case of indigenous peoples and local communities, assessments should be in accord with the guidelines adopted by the Conference of Parties to the Convention on Biological Diversity.»[34]

[31] BOYD, David R. op. cit., p. 17.

[32] *Idem, ibidem.*

[33] Idem, p. 18.

[34] KNOX, John H. UN. Human Rights Council. Special Rapporteur on the Issue of Human Rights Obligations Relating to the Enjoyment of a Safe, Clean, Healthy and Sustainable Environment UN. Human Rights Council. Secretariat (A/HRC/37/59) Geneve, UN, 24 Jan.

There is still a gap in Brazil between state commitments assumed by the country, rights enshrined in the constitutional text or infra-constitutional norms and reality. In procedural terms, for example, one must effectively implement: a) the right of access to information, since there is evidence that «the government faces difficulties in fulfilling commitments for greater transparency in the area of monitoring on climate change»[35] ; b) indigenous rights, which have been systematically violated in Brazil according to the Report of Violence against the Indigenous Peoples of Brazil data from 2019.[36] In substantial terms, the state's duty of not violating the right to a safe climate requires taking action in order to stabilize the Earth's climate, which means that in the case of Brazil for example, includes applying an effective policy to protect the Amazon rainforest, whose deforestation grew by 22% in 2021, according to INPE[37] and the «*acclimatization*» of public policies and legal instruments in a transversal way and in different scales. Finally, in terms of specific measures directed towards the most vulnerable and, in particular, to those in the coastal zone, there is a need for integrated studies on the vulnerability of Brazilian coastal cities[38], mitigating and adaptation measures that should consider the integrity of the coastal ecosystem from the point of view of the existing relationship between climate change and biodiversity.

2018, p. 17 Available at: <https://digitallibrary.un.org/record/1474985?ln=en> Access 20 Dec. 2021.

[35] RIBEIRO, Ingrid. LAI 10 anos: governo enfrenta dificuldades em cumprir transparência de dados sobre mudanças climáticas. O Globo 18.Nov.2021. Available at: https://oglobo.globo.com/brasil/meio-ambiente/lai-10-anos-governo-enfrenta-dificuldades-em-cumprir-transparencia-de-dados-sobre-mudancas-climaticas-25282304 Access on 20 Dec 2021.

[36] CIMI. Relatório Violência contra os Povos Indígenas do Brasil. Available at https://cimi.org.br/2020/09/em-2019-terras-indigenas-invadidas-modo-ostensivo-brasil/ Access 20 Dec. 2021.

[37] SALOMAO, Marta. O governo sabia (e não contou). Piauí, 18.Nov.2021. Available at: < https://piaui.folha.uol.com.br/o-governo-sabia-e-nao-contou/> Access 20 Dec. 2021.

[38] According to Adapta Clima, a knowledge platform on adaptation to climate change of the Ministry of the Environment «Brazil still does not have an integrated study of the vulnerability of coastal cities to the impacts resulting from climate change on a national scale, particularly in relation to relative sea level rise (PBMC, 2017)» (Free translation) MMA. AdaptaCLIMA – Zonas costeiras no contexto da mudança do clima. Available at: < http://adaptaclima.mma.gov.br/zonas-costeiras> Access on 20 Dec 2021.

3. Climate change and biodiversity protection in the coastal zone

The inability to maintain a temperature rise within levels of 1,5ºC according to expectation in the Paris Agreement, from conventional measures to reduce greenhouse gas emissions highlights technological solutions. However, in addition to those technological solutions, there are others which nature provides and are often either unknown or underestimated. In fact, both terrestrial and marine ecosystems play an important role in the carbon cycle.

Nature-Based Solutions (NBS) can be defined as «actions to protect, sustainably manage, and restore natural or modified ecosystems, that address societal challenges effectively and adaptively, simultaneously providing human well-being and biodiversity benefits». [39] Thus, the NBS seek to explain the positive link between solutions for society and nature.[40] However, NBS can also be defined from an innovation perspective: the European Commission has adopted NBS as part of the Horizon 2020 research program and is investing in projects to reinforce NBS-based evidence.[41]

The NBS became a fundamental element within the mitigation and adaptation strategy in the fight against climate change: these solutions can, simultaneously, able biodiversity preservation and fight against the negative effects of climate change.

However, there are overlapping occurrences around this concept with others, such as «Ecosystem-Based Adaptation/Mitigation» as can be observed in the following table

[39] IUCN. WCC Resolution 069 *Defining Nature-based Solutions* 2016. Available at: <https://portals.iucn.org/library/sites/library/files/resrecfiles/WCC_2016_RES_069_EN.pdf> Access 20 Dec. 2021.

[40] NESSHÖVER, Carsten et al. The science, policy and practice of nature-based solutions: an interdisciplinary perspective. In *Science of the Total Environment* 579, 2017, p. 1215-1227.

[41] MAES, Joachim; SANDER, Jacobs. Nature-Based Solutions for Europe's Sustainable Development. In *Conservation Letters*, 10(1), January/February 2017, pp. 121–124.

TABLE I – **«Nature-Based Solutions (NBS)» & «Ecosystem-Based Adaptation/Mitigation»**

Concept	«Nature-Based Solutions (NBS)»	«Ecosystem-Based Adaptation/Mitigation»
Definition	«actions to protect, sustainably manage, and restore natural or modified ecosystems, that address societal challenges effectively and adaptively, simultaneously providing human well-being and biodiversity benefits» (IUCN, 2016).	'The adaptation policies and measures that take into account the role of ecosystem services in reducing the vulnerability of society to climate change, in a multi-sectoral and multi-scale approach. EBA involves national and regional governments, local communities, private companies and NGOs in addressing the different pressures on ecosystem services, including land use change and climate change, and managing ecosystems to increase the resilience of people and economic sectors to climate change' (Vignola et al., 2009, p. 692).
Aim of employing concept	– provide effective solutions to major global challenges, – deliver clear biodiversity benefits in terms of diverse, well-managed and functioning ecosystems, – cost efficient relative to other solutions. – reach beyond the conservation community they need to be easily and compellingly communicated as well as being measurable, verifiable and replicable. – designed and implemented in such a way as to respect and reinforce communities' rights over natural resources.' (UCN, 2012. The IUCN Global Programme 2013–16, Adopted by the IUCN World Conservation Congress, September 2012, p. 16)	– reduce society's vulnerability to climate change (Vignola et al., 2009).
Potential relation	EBA should be part of NBS, to ensure solutions are climate-adapted.	

Source: Adapted from NESSHÖVER, Carsten et al. (2017)

So what is the main purpose of NBS? In fact, this concept was developed precisely to regroup, within the same range, a multiplicity of close concepts and actions related to them, such as

> «ecosystem-based adaptation, green infrastructures, the reduction of catastrophic risks based upon ecosystems, ecosystem services, ecological engineering. The NBS concept gives room for greater visibility to all these scattered concepts and thus make a united front against the dominant weight of conventional engineering solutions»[42]

According to the Global Standard for Nature-based Solutions (NBS) document from IUCN,

> «Research highlights that NbS could provide around 30% of the cost--effective mitigation needed by 2030 to stabilise warming to below 2°C. They can also provide a powerful defence against the impacts and long-term hazards of climate change, which is the biggest threat to biodiversity. Finding ways to work with ecosystems, rather than relying solely on conventional engineered solutions, can help communities adapt to climate change impacts. Using nature to green cities can also result in significant energy savings and health benefits»[43].

There is an association between NBS and mitigation legal instruments and adaptation to the effects of climate change: these solutions have been outlined in the Nationally Determined Contributions (NDCs) – a climate action plan to cut emissions and adapt to climate impacts, considered in the Paris Agreement – of which participating States must submit regularly and review every 5 (five) years.[44] The NDCs are key element in the Paris Agreement.

[42] ONEREC. Des Solutions fondées sur la Nature pour s'adapter au changement climatique. Rapport de l'Onerc au Premier ministre et au Parlement La Documentation française : Paris, 2019, p. 7.

[43] IUCN. *Global Standard for Nature-based Solutions. A user-friendly framework for the verification, design and scaling up of NbS*. First edition. Gland, Switzerland: IUCN, 2020. Available at: < https://portals.iucn.org/library/sites/library/files/documents/2020-020-En.pdf> Access 20 Dec. 2021.

[44] Arts. 4.3 and 4.9 of the Paris Agreement.

When assessing the inclusion of the NBS in NDCs based on conducted research it is noticed that in the case of blue carbon ecosystems – mangroves, tidal saltmarshes, and seagrasses: a) in 2016 it was observed that in 151 countries: «28 countries' NDCs include a reference to coastal wetlands in terms of mitigation, 59 countries include coastal ecosystems and the coastal zone into their adaptation strategies»[45]; b) in 2021 it was found that between March 29, 2019 and June 8, 2021, 63 countries submitted or updated their NDCs, of which 33 included coastal and marina NBS in their new or updated NDCs. [46] There is also indication of the necessity to ensure reinforced transparency, adopted by the Paris Agreement. [47]

Note that in the case of the coastal zone it is observed that the conservation and sustainable management of the coastal and marine ecosystems contribute in terms of climate change adaptation, while

> «only three main ecosystems, namely salt marshes, mangroves, and seagrasses have a quantifiable mitigation contribution with internationally-approved accounting guidance and methodologies from the IPCC. These three ecosystems are often called coastal 'blue carbon ecosystems' for their ability to contribute to climate mitigation»[48].

Can the NBS concept be understood as an opportunity to engage the States and other actors in a societal change process of recognizing nature's role? In order for this to occur, Seddon et al. proposes four principles to ensure the sustainable development of contemporary societies:

[45] Herr, D; Landis, E. *Coastal blue carbon ecosystems. Opportunities for Nationally Determined Contributions. Policy Brief.* Gland, Switzerland: IUCN and Washington, DC, USA: TNC, 2016, p. 6.

[46] Lecerf, M.; Herr, D.; Thomas, T.; Elverum, C.; Delrieu, E.; Picourt, L.. Coastal and marine ecosystems as Nature-based Solutions in new or updated Nationally Determined Contributions, Ocean & Climate Platform, Conservation International, IUCN, GIZ, Rare, The Nature Conservancy and WWF, 2021.

[47] Art. 13 Paris Agreement.

[48] GLOBAL CLIMATE ACTION/MARRAKECH PARTNERSHIP. Climate Action Pathway Oceans and Coastal Zones – Action Table. 2020. Available at: < https://unfccc.int/sites/default/files/resource/Action_table%20_OCZ.pdf> Access 20 Dec. 2021.

«(i) NbS are not a substitute for the rapid phase out of fossil fuels;

(ii) NbS involve a wide range of ecosystems on land and in the sea, not just forests; (iii) NbS are implemented with the full engagement and consent of Indigenous Peoples and local communities in a way that respects their cultural and ecological rights; and

(iv) NbS should be explicitly designed to provide measurable benefits for biodiversity»[49]

In 2020, the IUCN adopted a standard which aims to clarify and require not only the concept of NBS but also its potential for building a fair and sustainable world, based on 8 criteria and 28 indicators. The eight criteria are: (i) NBS effectively address societal challenges, (ii) design of NBS is informed by scale, (iii) NBS result in a net gain to biodiversity and ecosystem integrity, (iv) NBS are economically viable, (v) NBS are based on inclusive, transparent and empowering governance process, (vi) NBS equitably balance trade-offs between achievement of their primary goal(s) and the continued provision of multiple benefits, (vii) NBS are managed adaptively, based on evidence, (viii) NBS are sustainable and mainstreamed within an appropriate jurisdictional context.[50]

And so, societal changes and the impacts upon the most vulnerable population in coastal cities must be taken into consideration when endorsing NBS, identifying the benefits for the biodiversity, the integrity of the ecosystem and the human population. The integrated management of coastal zone and coastal ecosystem conservation and sustainable urban planning[51], for example, can be an instrument which considers NBS, highlighting the role of dunes and mangroves, as well as residing traditional populations that reside there. As pointed out in the *Relatório Mudanças Climáticas e Cidades*, the mangroves represent an ecosystem that

[49] SEDDON, Nathalie et al. Getting the message right on nature-based solutions to climate change. In *Global Change Biology* vol. 27, 8, 2021, pp. 1518-1546.

[50] IUCN. *Global Standard for Nature-based Solutions. A user-friendly framework for the verification, design and scaling up of NbS*. First edition. Gland, Switzerland: IUCN, 2020. Available at: < https://portals.iucn.org/library/sites/library/files/documents/2020-020-En.pdf> Access 20 Dec. 2021.

[51] DE LUCA, Claudia, et al. Nature-Based Solutions and Sustainable Urban Planning in the European Environmental Policy Framework: Analysis of the State of the Art and Recommendations for Future Development. In *Sustainability* 13/2021, 5021.

provides several benefits to the environment, and even though they are present on almost the entire Brazilian coast and there are many studies indicating that the «maintenance of healthy urban ecosystems is an important tool to increase the resilience of cities (...). [But.] (u)nfortunately, the vast majority of cities have not yet developed climate change adaptation strategies»[52]. Only «cities such as Santos, Rio de Janeiro and Recife have already started vulnerability studies and adaptation plans for climate change».[53]

In IPCC evaluations a key conclusion regarding coastal systems indicate that «reactive and standalone efforts to reduce climate-related risks to coastal systems are less effective than responses which are part of integrated coastal zone management (ICZM), including long-term national and community planning»[54]. In that sense, the integrated management of coastal zone and the sustainable urban planning occupy a prominent spot, considering a process in which the social and environmental benefits are equitably distributed.

Final considerations

The necessary changes in human activities in order to limit global warming to 1,5ºC are certainly unprecedented and will be possible only if there is a transformation in how human activities are developed considering the impoverished so that they are not the most affected. Therefore, a safe climate works as a vital element for the right to an ecologically balanced environment and essential for human well-being and for life. Ensuring that in different levels there are necessary measures being taken in order to fight against the nefarious effects of climate change is a necessity and permeates the understanding of concepts such as vulnerability, equity and climate justice, especially in coastal cities where the majority of the human population resides in the world and also in Brazil.

[52] RIBEIRO, Suzana Kahn; SANTOS, Andrea Souza (eds.). Mudanças Climáticas e Cidades: Relatório Especial do Painel Brasileiro de Mudanças Climáticas. PBMC, COPPE – UFRJ, Rio de Janeiro, p. 38. Available at: <http://www.pbmc.coppe.ufrj.br/documentos/Relatorio_UM_v10-2017-1.pdf Access 20 Dec. 2021.

[53] MMA. AdaptaCLIMA – Zonas costeiras no contexto da mudança do clima. Available at: < http://adaptaclima.mma.gov.br/zonas-costeiras> Access on 20 Dec 2021.

[54] https://www.ipcc.ch/site/assets/uploads/2018/02/ar4-wg2-chapter6-1.pdf

The relationship between human rights and climate change can be considered a clue for implementing the rights of the most vulnerable in face of climate change effects, taking into account different levels such as health, education and transportation, but also the right to a sustainable present-future. In that sense, emerging concepts like NBS should be analyzed, indicating its potential to simultaneously provide tools to fight climate change and biodiversity loss. However, trending concepts must be analyzed with caution by observing which parameters are used in order to achieve their goals, or, in other words, to effectively provide the necessary changes for the construction of a fairer and sustainable world.

References

BERENGUER, Erika et. al. Drivers and Ecological Impacts of Deforestation and Forest Degradation. In SCIENCE PANEL FOR THE AMAZON. Amazon Assessment Report 2021. Available at: https://www.theamazonwewant.org/amazon-assessment-report-2021/ Access 20 Dec. 2021.

BODANSKY, Daniel. Introduction: climate change and human rights: unpacking the issues. In *Georgia Journal of International and Comparative Law* vol. 38, n. 3, 2010, pp. 511-524.

BOYD, David R. UN Human Rights Council Special Rapporteur on the Issue of Human Rights Obligations Relating to the Enjoyment of a Safe, Clean, Healthy and Sustainable Environment (A/74/161), New York, 15 July 2019, p. 5. Available at: < https://digitallibrary.un.org/record/3814570> Access 20 Dec. 2021.

BRASIL. Decreto n. 5.300, de 7 de dezembro de 2004, que regulamenta a Lei n. 7.661, de 16 de maio de 1988, que institui o Plano Nacional de Gerenciamento Costeiro – PNGC, dispõe sobre regras de uso e ocupação da zona costeira e estabelece critérios de gestão da orla marítima, e dá outras providências.

CIMI. Relatório Violência contra os Povos Indígenas do Brasil. Available at https://cimi.org.br/2020/09/em-2019-terras-indigenas-invadidas-modo-ostensivo--brasil/ Access 20 Dec. 2021.

COURNIL, Christel. Introduction. In COURNIL, Christel (dir.) *La fabrique d'un droit climatique: au service de la trajectoire '1.5'*. Paris: Pedone, 2021.

COMMUNIQUÉ REGARDING THE FULFILLMENT BY THE BRAZILIAN GOVERNMENT OF ILO CONVENTION 169 ADDRESSING INDIGENOUS AND TRIBAL PEOPLES, 2018. Available at: < https://cpisp.org.br/wp-content/uploads/2018/09/Comm uniqueRegar dingtheFulfillme ntBytheBrazilianGovernmentofiloConvention169AddressingIndigenousandTribalPeoples_2008.pdf> Access 20 Dec. 2021.

DE LUCA, Claudia, et al. Nature-Based Solutions and Sustainable Urban Planning in the European Environmental Policy Framework: Analysis of the State of the Art and Recommendations for Future Development. In *Sustainability* 13/2021, 5021.

Global Carbon Project. *Global Carbon Atlas 2021*. Available at: http://www.globalcarbonatlas.org/en/content/welcome-carbon-atlas Access 20 Dec. 2021.

GLOBAL CLIMATE ACTION/MARRAKECH PARTNERSHIP. Climate Action Pathway Oceans and Coastal Zones – Action Table. 2020. Available at: < https://unfccc.int/sites/default/files/resource/Action_table%20_OCZ.pdf> Access 20 Dec. 2021.

Herr, D; Landis, E. *Coastal blue carbon ecosystems. Opportunities for Nationally Determined Contributions. Policy Brief.* Gland, Switzerland: IUCN and Washington, DC, USA: TNC, 2016.

Houghton, John Theodore; Jenkins, G.J.; Ephraums J.J.,(eds). *Climate Change: The IPCC Scientific Assessment*, 1990. Group I. IPCC, Cambridge, UK: Cambridge Univ. Press, 1993.

HUMANS RIGHTS COUNCIL. Climate change and poverty – Report of the Special Rapporteur on extreme poverty and human rights (A/HRC/41/39), 17 July 2019, p. 4. Available at: < https://undocs.org/en/A/HRC/41/39> Access 20 Dec. 2021.

IBGE. Municípios defrontantes com o mar 2020. Disponível em: < https://geoftp.ibge.gov.br/organizacao_do_territorio/estrutura_territorial/municipios_defrontantes_com_o_mar/2020/Municipios_Defrontantes_com_o_Mar_2020.pdf> Acesso em 22.10.2021.

IOC – Intergovernmental Oceanographic Commission. *Hazard awareness and risk mitigation in integrated coastal area management. United Nations Educational, Scientific and Cultural Organization (UNESCO)*, Manuals and Guides No 50, ICAM Dossier No 5, 141p., Paris, França, 2009. Available at: <http://legacy.ioc-unesco.org/index.php?option=com_oe&task=viewDocumentRecord&docID=3947> Access 20 Dec. 2021.

IUCN. *Global Standard for Nature-based Solutions. A user-friendly framework for the verification, design and scaling up of NbS*. First edition. Gland, Switzerland: IUCN, 2020. Available at: < https://portals.iucn.org/library/sites/library/files/documents/2020-020-En.pdf> Access 20 Dec. 2021.

IUCN. WCC Resolution 069 *Defining Nature-based Solutions* 2016. Available at: <https://portals.iucn.org/library/sites/library/files/resrecfiles/WCC_2016_RES_069_EN.pdf> Access 20 Dec. 2021.

IWAMA, Allan Yu et al. Risk, Vulnerability and Adaptation to Climate Change: an Interdisciplinary Approach. In Ambie. Soc. 19 (2), Apr-Jun 2016. Available at: < https://doi.org/10.1590/1809-4422ASOC137409V1922016> Access 20 Dec. 2021.

KNOX, John H. UN. Human Rights Council. Special Rapporteur on the Issue of Human Rights Obligations Relating to the Enjoyment of a Safe, Clean, Healthy and Sustainable Environment UN. Human Rights Council. Secretariat (A/HRC/37/59) Geneve, UN, 24 Jan. 2018, p. 17 Available at: <https://digitallibrary.un.org/record/1474985?ln=en> Access 20 Dec. 2021.

Lecerf, M.; Herr, D.; Thomas, T.; Elverum, C.; Delrieu, E.; Picourt, L.. Coastal and marine ecosystems as Nature-based Solutions in new or updated Nationally Determined Contributions, Ocean & Climate Platform, Conservation International, IUCN, GIZ, Rare, The Nature Conservancy and WWF, 2021.

LEROY, Jean Pierre. 2009. Justiça climática: um direito humano negado. In *Democracia Viva* n. 43, 2009.

MAES, Joachim; SANDER, Jacobs. Nature-Based Solutions for Europe's Sustainable Development. In *Conservation Letters*, 10(1), January/February 2017, pp. 121–124.

MARENGO, José A.; SCARANO, Fabio R. (eds.) Impacto, vulnerabilidade e adaptação das cidades costeiras brasileiras às mudanças climáticas. Relatório Especial do Painel Brasileiro de Mudanças Climáticas. PBMC, COPPE – UFRJ, 2016, p. 132. Disponível em <https://ppgoceano.paginas.ufsc.br/files/2017/06/Relatorio_DOIS_v1_04.06.17.pdf> Access 20 Dec. 2021.

MBOYA, Atieno. Vulnerability and the Climate Change Regime. In *UCLA Journal of Environmental Law and Policy,* 36 (1), 2018, pp. 79-103.

McLNERNEY-LANKFORD, Siobhán, DARROW, Mac, RAJAMANI, Lavanya. Human rights and climate change: a review of the international legal dimensions. Washington: World Bank, 2011.

MMA. AdaptaCLIMA – Zonas costeiras no contexto da mudança do clima. Available at: < http://adaptaclima.mma.gov.br/zonas-costeiras> Access on 20 Dec 2021.

NESSHÖVER, Carsten et al. The science, policy and practice of nature-based solutions: an interdisciplinary perspective. In *Science of the Total Environment* 579, 2017, p. 1215-1227.

NICOLADI, Joao Luiz; PETERMANN, Rafael Mueller. Mudanças climáticas e a Vulnerabilidade da Zona Costeira do Brasil: Aspectos ambientais, sociais e tecnológicos. In *Revista de Gestão Costeira,* 10(2), 2010, p. 153. Available at: < https://www.aprh.pt/rgci/pdf/rgci-206_Nicolodi.pdf> Access 20 Dec. 2021.

ONEREC. Des Solutions fondées sur la Nature pour s'adapter au changement climatique. Rapport de l'Onerc au Premier ministre et au Parlement La Documentation française : Paris, 2019.

RIBEIRO, Ingrid. LAI 10 anos: governo enfrenta dificuldades em cumprir transparência de dados sobre mudanças climáticas. O Globo 18.Nov.2021. Available at: https://oglobo.globo.com/brasil/meio-ambiente/lai-10-anos-governo-enfrenta-dificuldades-em-cumprir-transparencia-de-dados-sobre-mudancas-climaticas-25282304 Access on 20 Dec 2021.

RIBEIRO, Suzana Kahn; SANTOS, Andrea Souza (eds.). Mudanças Climáticas e Cidades: Relatório Especial do Painel Brasileiro de Mudanças Climáticas. PBMC, COPPE – UFRJ, Rio de Janeiro, p. 38. Available at: <http://www.pbmc.coppe.ufrj.br/documentos/Relatorio_UM_v10-2017-1.pdf Access 20 Dec. 2021.

SALOMAO, Marta. O governo sabia (e não contou). Piauí, 18.Nov.2021. Available at: < https://piaui.folha.uol.com.br/o-governo-sabia-e-nao-contou/> Access 20 Dec. 2021.

SEDDON, Nathalie et al. Getting the message right on nature-based solutions to climate change. In *Global Change Biology* vol. 27, 8, 2021, pp. 1518-1546.

SILVA, Solange Teles da; RAMOS, Marina C. . Justiça climática: desafios e perspectivas a partir de uma análise das decisões dos Tribunais Superiores Brasileiros. In: AYALA, Patryck. (Org.). *O Direito das mudanças climáticas: normatividade e princípios para a justiça ecológica no direito nacional e internacional.* 1ed.Curitiba: CRV, 2020, v. 1, p. 77-96.

UNFCCC. Decision 1/CP. 16 The Cancun Agreements: Outcome of the work of the Ad Hoc Working Group on Long-term Cooperative Action under the Convention.

UNFCCC. Policy Brief Technologies for Averting, Minimizing and Addressing Loss and Damage in Coastal Zone. Executive Committee of the Warsaw International Mechanism for Loss and Damage – Technology Executive Committee, 2020, p. 16. Available at: < https://unfccc.int/ttclear/misc_/StaticFiles/gnwoerk_static/2020_coastalzones/b9e88f6fea374d8aa5cb44115d201160/3863c9fabdf74ea49710189acbf6907a.pdf> Access 20 Dec. 2021.

UNGA. Human rights obligations relating to the enjoyment of a safe, clean, healthy and sustainable environment – Report of the Special Rapporteur John H. Knox, (A/73/188), 19 July 2018. Available at: <https://undocs.org/en/A/73/188 > Access 20 Dec. 2021.

2. ELADIO DIESTE'S INVENTIVE DESIGN AND BUILD – THE DISCONTINUOUS GAUSSIAN VAULTS

Felipe Corres Melachos
Wilson Florio
Federica Maietti
Luca Rossato

> Eladio Dieste addressed the transformation of an architectural poetics through the path of a clear, precise, and simple building technique. The idea that technical clarity, precision, and simplicity would lead almost naturally to artistic production also underlies the work of men such as Nervi, Fuller, and Candela. It constitutes an answer, in a sense symmetrical and, in a sense, opposite, to the attitude of the men of the rationalist decade, who discovered the importance of being good builders when they were already good architects. The men of the 30s started with theoretical, almost academic, explorations of architectural values [...] Those who, like Dieste, resorted to the opposite path: starting by building, they discovered architecture [...] (BONTA, 1963, p. 9, translation by the authors)

Introduction

This chapter aims to explain the methodological procedures and results of the Ph.D. thesis *Parametric Modelling of Dieste's Gaussian Vaults*, developed by one of the authors of these writings – Prof. Dr. Felipe Corres Melachos. This thesis was the fruit of a double degree from Mackenzie Presbyterian University and Università degli Studi di Ferrara, in which the supervisors were Prof. Dr. Wilson Florio, Prof. Dr. Federica Maietti, and Prof. Dr. Luca Rossato. This thesis was approved with distinction by the board in 2020, having received honors such as *Highlight Thesis of the Quadrennium* from PPGAU-Fau Mackenzie in 2021 and the *Honorable Mention of the 2021 CAPES Thesis Award* in the area of Architecture, Urbanism, and Design.

The explorations that resulted in this work fit the *Modern and Contemporary Architecture, representation, and intervention* research line of the Post-Graduate Program of the School of Architecture and Urbanism of Mackenzie University. It is also important to mention that this work was only made possible thanks to the financial support of CAPES. This financial support made the stay in Ferrara, Italy, possible so the authors could use the technology tools and didactic support from the co-supervisors from the partner institution, Università degli Studi di Ferrara. Thus, this work is inserted in the Institutional Internationalization Program, the CAPES – PRINT, at Mackenzie Presbyterian University, under the tutelage of Prof. Dr. Wilson Florio.

The object of study of this research was the discontinuous Gaussian vaults (Figure 1), dominant variation of the typology of Gaussian vaults designed and built by the Uruguayan engineer Eladio Dieste (1917-2000). These discontinuous Gaussian vaults differ from the continuous Gaussian vaults (Figure 2) regarding the presence of zenithal openings that resemble sheds. Eladio Dieste was often helped by local architects to better contextualize and adapt his work.

Gaussian vaults are a structural typology of unprecedented and original authorship by engineer Eladio Dieste. Dieste himself defines the Gaussian vaults by the five technical-constructive design assumptions below, highlighting the importance of geometry in the result, as well as the use of a minimum of material (especially hardware) as a mechanism to achieve large spans:

1. The brick – mortar – steel assembly behaves like a structurally viable unit. This was the basic premise from which one could begin to think and sense the subsequent solution.
2. We chose the catenary as a guideline so that the proper weight of the structure produces simple compression and makes the structure resist bending efforts. This capacity significantly increases if we consider a 'minimum amount of constructive' reinforcement.
3. Compression efforts from the weight of the structure itself are not dependent on the section [...] However, the magnitude of these

efforts is low: in a vault with a span of 100 m and a sag of 10 m, compression is 27 kg/cm3, assuming a specific weight of 2 tons/m3.
4. The minimum reinforcement ensures that the longitudinal axis of the shell [...] reacts as an elastic unit against the concentrated loads.
5. Bearing in mind that the only material to harden is the joints and that the mixture's trace causes the mortar to quickly gather enough strength [...] to break down the vault before the mortar has completely hardened. This has been confirmed by tests, not only for small vaults but for large structures. (DIESTE *in* TORRECILLAS, 1996, p. 41, translation by the authors).

FIGURE 1: **Examples of discontinuous Gaussian vaults.**

a

Figure 1.a: Internal view of the discontinuous Gaussian vaults of the CEASA in Porto Alegre, designed and built between 1968 and 1972 by Eladio Dieste, together with architects Carlos Maximiliano Fayet and Claudio Araujo.
Source: MELACHOS, Felipe Corres. 1 photo. 2018.

FIGURE 1: **Examples of discontinuous Gaussian vaults (continued).**

b

c

(Fig. 1.b) External side view of the discontinuous Gaussian vaults of the Montevideo Port Warehouse, projected and built between 1977 and 1979; (Fig. 1.c) External front view of the discontinuous Gaussian vaults of Lanas Trinidad Warehouse, built in Durazno between 1988 and 1990, and enlarged between 1991 and 1993.
Source: (Fig. 1.c) FLORIO, Wilson. 1 photo. 2017; (Fig. 1.c.) FINOTTI, Leonardo. 1 photo. 2016.

FIGURE 2: **The continuous Gaussian vaults of the Cristo Obrero Church in Atlantida (Uruguay), designed and built between 1952 and 1960 by Eladio Dieste.**

a

b

Source: (Fig. 2.a) MELACHOS, Felipe Corres. 1 photo. 2018; (Fig. 2.b) FINOTTI, Leonardo. 1 photo. 2011.

Consequently, the chronological and geographic clippings of the research are focused on the design and construction location and time of the discontinuous Gaussian vaults by Eladio Dieste. The time was between 1955 and 2000, and the locations were the territories of Uruguay, Brazil, Argentina, and Spain.

The problem of this research came from the lack of knowledge about Eladio Dieste's work and the work of other prominent figures within the inventiveness of construction technology in Latin America. This phenomenon caused Eladio Dieste to be left out of related academic explorations in the second half of the 20th century and the beginning of the 21st century. This scarcity of academic investigations contrasts with his contribution in the universe of construction technology, reinventing constructive procedures in reinforced ceramics, and generating new typologies for large spans such as Gaussian vaults and prestressing techniques for his self-supporting vaults (Figure 3).

FIGURE 3: **The self-supporting vaults at the multi-purpose Hall of Paroquia Santo Augustin, in Montevideo (Uruguay), currently a laboratory, designed and built between 1977 and 1980 by Eladio Dieste.**

Source: MELACHOS, Felipe Corres. 1 photo. 2018.

This absence of academic exploration has proved to be even more remarkable as the object of investigation is the geometry of the works of Eladio Dieste, especially concerning his Gaussian vaults and also using instruments of analysis based on parametric modeling. However, a significant stimulus for the study of Dieste's work was its inclusion in 2010 in UNESCO's Latin American Southern Cone and Spain indicative list (UNESCO, 2014), as well as the more extensive assessment of his works in Uruguay for UNESCO's listing in 2014 (UNESCO, 2014). Furthermore, in July 2021, the Cristo Obrero Church (Figure 2) was declared a UNESCO World Heritage Site (UNESCO, 2021).

Given this context, the central hypothesis of the doctoral thesis submitted established and proved that there is a set of underlying geometric relationships in roofs structured with discontinuous Gaussian vaults designed and built with reinforced ceramics by Eladio Dieste. As presented in the next section, the nature of the geometry of the objects studied evoked the use of parametric modeling as an analysis tool. This tool, in turn, allowed us to analyze this geometry in its resulting architectural space, in climatic facets, and its design and construction process.

Method

The method chosen for this research resulted in the study being structured on a theoretical and an empirical basis, called "research procedures" and "analysis procedures," as seen in Figure 4. On the theoretical basis, we exhausted the state-of-the-art about the object of study through extensive consultation of academic indexes such as *the Web-of-Science* and *the Avery Index*. In these academic indexes, the scarcity of academic exploration on the research theme was scientifically proven, and the nature and origin of the publications were verified, indicating the following steps to be taken in the research.

As presented in Figure 4, this bibliographic review was accompanied by visits to the works, universities, research centers, and libraries of interest in Uruguay, Brazil, and Spain. These visits allowed us to get closer to his work and obtain original drawings from Dieste & Montañez S.A., the current company of Dieste's heirs and former collaborators, and eventual partners in the development of works and designs. This material allowed for the development of the empirical basis of the research.

These original drawings, authorized only for non-profit publications, were obtained only thanks to the immeasurable help of the team of researchers and professors at Udelar (*Universidad de la Republica de Uruguay*), whose names we will not mention so as not to run the risk of incurring an indecorous omission of credit.

FIGURE 4: **Summary of the methodological procedures of the research conducted.**

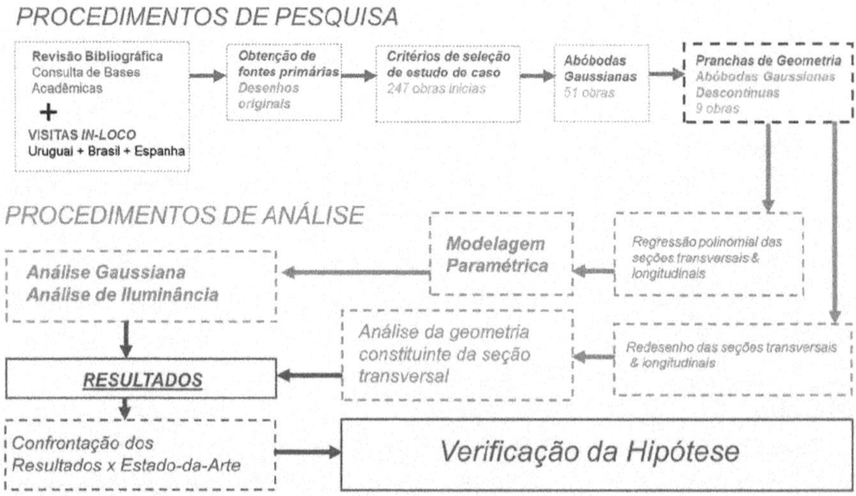

Source: MELACHOS, Felipe Corres. 1 diagram. 2019.

Through these drawings, one can map the trajectory of the Uruguayan engineer in several facets, such as his production per year and typology (5.a). These primary sources also allowed for determining the case studies through the availability of *geometry boards,* which contained the constructive and geometric data of the designs' discontinuous Gaussian vaults. Details of these boards appear redrawn in Figure 5.b.

The understanding of these *geometry boards* was obtained through analysis procedures, such as redrawing them (Fig. 5.b), and later polynomial regression by the method of least squares (MENDENHALL;

BEAVER; BEAVER, 2006) of the curves resulting from each cross and longitudinal section of the Gaussian vaults in the *Microsoft Excel* (Fig. 5.c) and *R* software. The closer the value of "R^2" is to 1, the more reliable the polynomial resulting from the analysis will be.

FIGURE 5: **Data collected from primary sources and initial exploratory analyzes.**

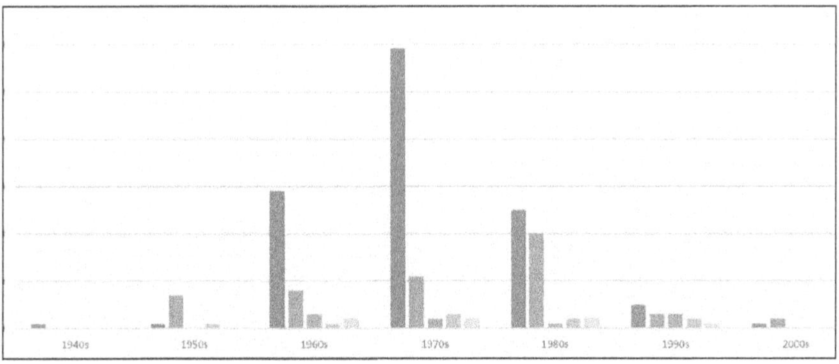

a

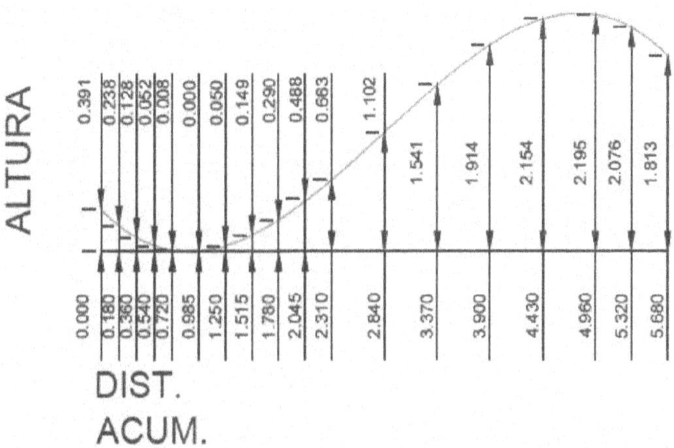

b

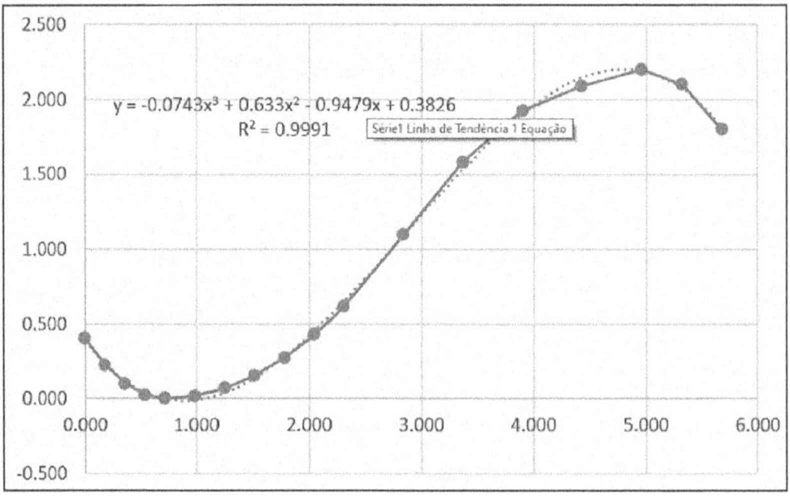

c

Figure 5.a: Eladio Dieste's production by decade and structural typology. Caption: Blue – Self-supporting vaults; Orange – Gaussian vaults; Gray – Ruled surfaces and bent plates; Yellow – Horizontal silos; Pink – Towers and reservoirs; Fig. 5.b: Redrawing of the cross--section of the Montevideo Port Warehouse from the primary sources; Fig. 5.c: Results of polynomial regression of the cross-section of the Montevideo Port Warehouse in Microsoft Excel.
Source: (Fig. 5.a) MELACHOS, Felipe Corres. 1 graph. 2019; (Fig. 5.b) Source: MELACHOS, Felipe Corres. 1 drawing. 2019; (Fig. 5.c). MELACHOS, Felipe Corres. 1 model. 2019.

This polynomial regression of the sections, in turn, resulted in polynomials for the cross-sectional and longitudinal sections of discontinuous Gaussian vaults and thus allowed for the parametric modeling of the sections (Fig. 6.a). Due to the curvy and complex nature of the Gaussian vaults chosen, we have decided to do the parametric modeling of both sections and surfaces, for which this tool has already proven to be friendly in previous experiments (FLORIO, 2009).

This parametric modeling step had an exploratory character and aimed at unveiling how the design and geometric constitution of the components of this structural typology were performed. Therefore, the coordinates of the points that constitute the key cross and longitudinal sections were interpolated through segments of circumference arcs tangent to each other.

The parametric modeling of the sections and surfaces covered by the case studies using the *Rhinoceros 3D* and its *Grasshopper plug-in* (Fig. 6.b and 6.c), and as well as the algorithm of the sections, were performed in an exploratory way, using the polynomials previously obtained through the drawings. Figure 6.b represents a diagram of the algorithm developed for the surfaces of the Gaussian vaults (Fig. 6.b).

In this algorithm, first, the cross (green grouping) and longitudinal (dark blue grouping) sections were established using the previously obtained polynomials, reading from left to right. Subsequently, their positions were adjusted using the sag of the cross section (dark purple grouping) and vertical guides to align the cross section height (salmon grouping). In the meantime, we also performed curvature tests in the sections (orange grouping).

FIGURE 6: **Experimental parametric modeling of the sections and surfaces of the objects of the study.**

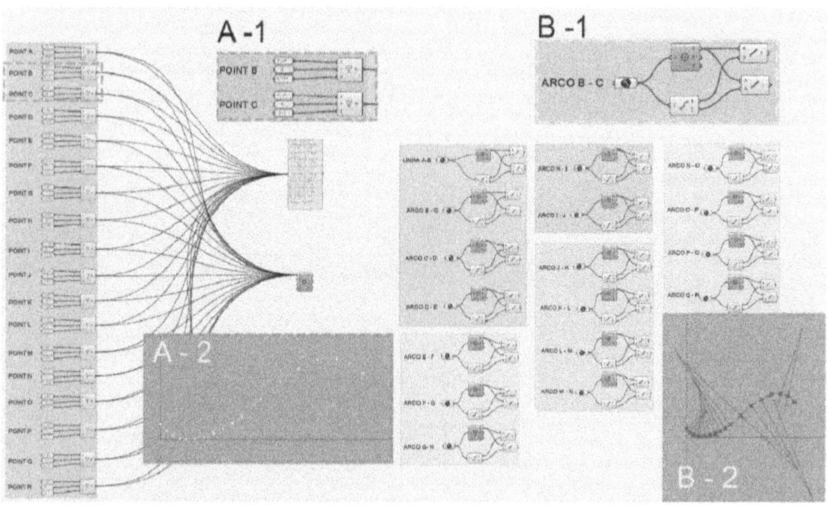

a

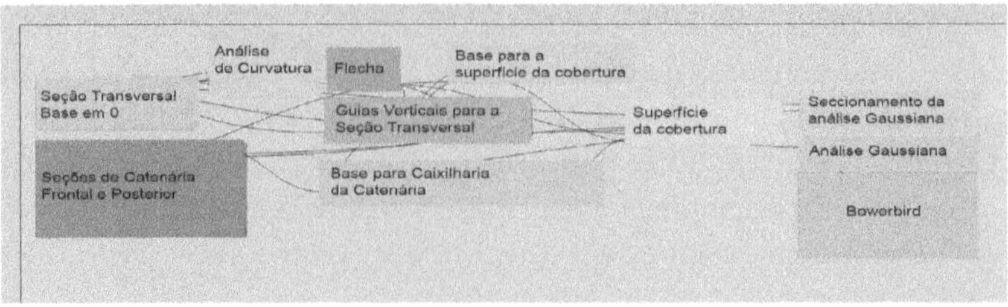

b

Figure 6.a: Parametric modeling of the cross sections; Fig. 6.b: Diagram of the parametric modeling algorithm of the surface of the Gaussian vaults of the Montevideo Port Warehouse. Source: (Fig. 6.a) MELACHOS, Felipe Corres. 1 model. 2018; (Fig. 6.b) MELACHOS, Felipe Corres. 1 algorithm. 2018.

Source: (Fig. 6.a) MELACHOS, Felipe Corres. 1 model. 2018; (Fig. 6.b; 6.c) MELACHOS, Felipe Corres. 1 algorithm. 2018.

FIGURE 6: **Experimental parametric modeling of the sections and surfaces of the objects of the study (continued).**

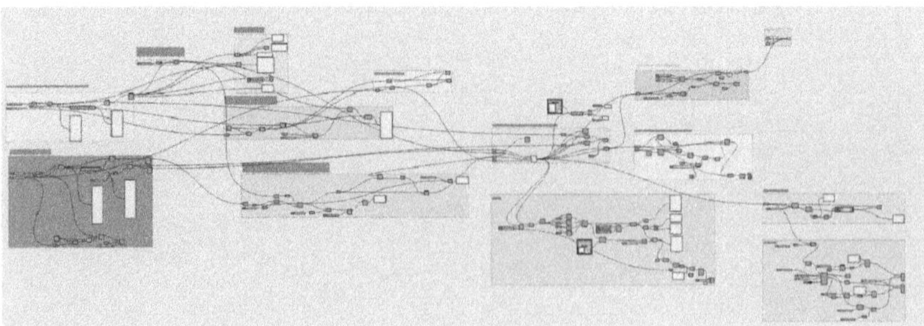

c

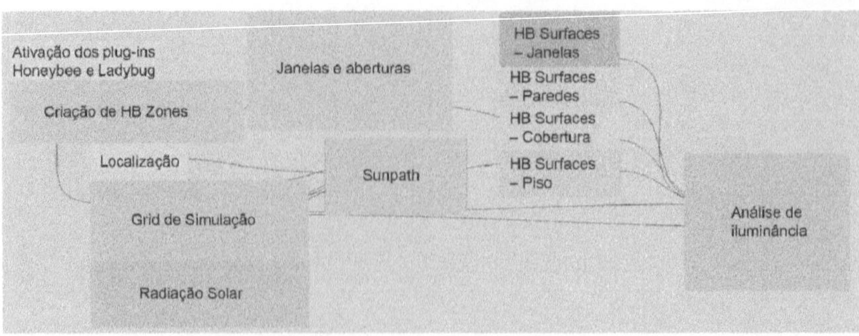

d

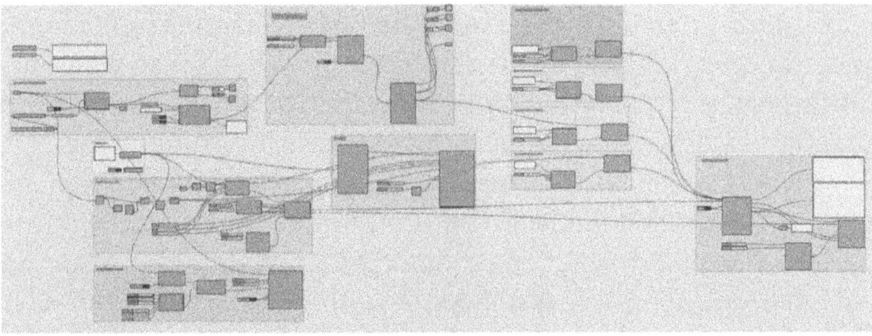

e

Figure 6.c: Parametric modeling algorithm of the surfaces of the Gaussian vaults of the Montevideo Port Warehouse; Fig. 6.d: Diagram of the illuminance analysis algorithm using the Parametric modeling of the interior resulting from the surface of the Gaussian vaults of the Montevideo Port Warehouse; Fig. 6.e: Illuminance analysis algorithm using the Parametric modeling of the interior resulting from the surfaces of the Gaussian vaults of the Montevideo Port Warehouse.
Source: (Fig. 6.c) MELACHOS, Felipe Corres. 1 algorithm. 2019; (Fig. 6.d; Fig. 6.e) MELACHOS, Felipe Corres. 1 algorithm. 2019.

The configuration of the final surface began by inserting the geometry of the frames that make this typology a "discontinuous" variation (light purple grouping) and the delimitation of a base for the roof (cyan grouping). Next, we modeled the surface of the roof (yellow grouping), defined the procedures for the Gaussian analysis of its surface (mustard and dark blue groupings), and made the preparation for later digital production via CNC (light green grouping) using the *Bowerbird plug-in*. The original algorithm (Fig. 6.c) also reveals experimentations with the positioning of the ceramic blocks on the surface (second light purple grouping) and other attempts to generate surfaces, also highlighted in light purple.

Finally, the case studies were submitted to illuminance analysis using parametric modeling, aiming to contemplate the object's architectural quality resulting from the geometry of the discontinuous Gaussian vaults in building roofs. The diagram of the illuminance algorithm (Fig. 6.d) demonstrates that we used the *Ladybug* and *Honeybee plug-ins*, the current versions of which still prompted their initial activation (yellow grouping).

The algorithm started (reading from left to right) with the creation of *Honeybee Zones* (purple grouping), so the geometry would be converted into tangible objects for *the plug-ins* used, the import of location climatic data (mustard grouping), and a basis for the simulations to be made (salmon grouping). These initial data have allowed for analyzing solar radiation (orange grouping) and solar trajectory (beige grouping) of each case study.

The algorithm's illuminance analysis would require all of its openings, so they were modeled (light green grouping) and transformed into *Honeybee surfaces* for analysis in the dark green groupings – windows, cyan – walls, pink – roof, and blue – floor. Finally, the illuminance analysis was performed and programmed for visualization (second salmon grouping).

As previously mentioned, the case studies that went through these parametric analysis processes were selected based on the availability of primary sources for their modeling. Therefore, the listing contemplates the buildings listed below:

1 – Caputto Factory, built in Salto (Uruguay) between 1971 and 1972 and expanded between 1986 and 1987.

2 – Montevideo Port Warehouse (also known as the Julio Herrera y Orbes Warehouse) (Uruguay), built between 1977 and 1979 (Fig. 7a and 7b).

3 – Ferrando Factory, built in Montevideo between 1979 and 1980.

4 – Tobacco Factory, built in Montevideo between 1969 and 1970, with expansions between 1980 and 1981, and 1982 and 1983.

5 – Hermanos Maristas School Gymnasium, built in Montevideo in 1982.

6 – Palenga Warehouse, built in Montevideo between 1981 and 1982. (Fig. 7c).

7 – Cin Cel Cur Factory, built in Montevideo in 1987.

8 – Fray Marcos Factory, built in Fray Marcos between 1986 and 1987, expanded between 1994 and 1995.

9 – Las Piedras Altas Warehouse and Factory, built in the Department of Florida between 1989 and 1990.

FIGURE 7: **Images of some of the selected case studies.**

a

b

(Fig. 7.a) External side view of the discontinuous Gaussian vaults of the Montevideo Port Warehouse, projected and built between 1977 and 1979. (Fig. 7.b) Internal view of the same project.
Source: (Fig. 7.a) FINOTTI, Leonardo. 1 photo. 2016; (Fig. 7.b.) FINOTTI, Leonardo. 1 photo. 2011.

FIGURE 7: **Images of some of the selected case studies (continued)**

c

(Fig. 7.c) External view of the Palenga Warehouse's Gaussian vaults.
Source: (Fig. 7-c) FINOTTI, Leonardo. 1 photo. 2016.

Results and Analyses

The results and analyzes of this research can be divided into three macro--categories: sections, surface, and illuminance. Concerning the sections, the results can be separated between the key cross and longitudinal sections.

In the scope of the cross sections, we found that, in the Gaussian vaults, their geometry was represented by the accumulated heights and distances marked on the "geometry boards." We also verified that this geometry could be approximated by circumference arcs tangent to each other or connected in the central portion of the curve by a straight segment (Table 1).

TABLE 01: **Analysis of the geometry that constitutes the key cross section.**

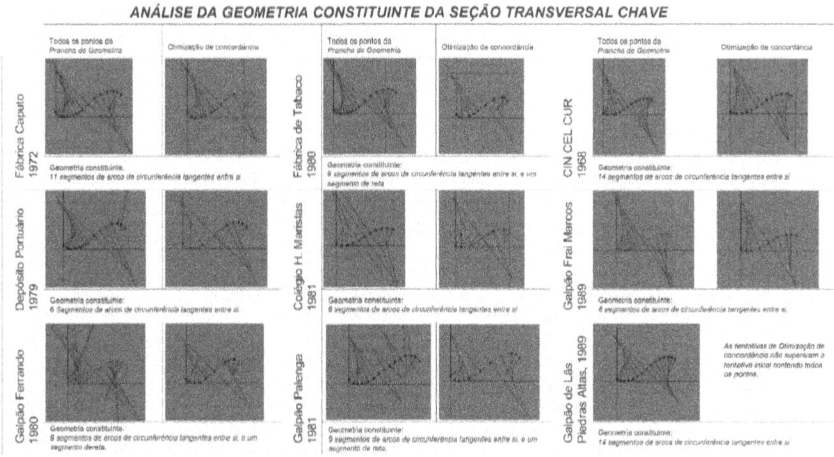

Source: MELACHOS, Felipe Corres. 1 table. 2018.

The redrawing of these sections demonstrated that their sags are variable and directly proportional to the transverse span, varying by approximately 67%. The sag dimensions recorded for this typology were 1.40 meters to 2.35 meters, and the proportions pf the sag-to-span ratio were 1 to 2 and 1 to 4.

Another significant result to be mentioned is that both cross and longitudinal sections of the discontinuous Gaussian vaults can be represented by polynomials (Table 2). The polynomial regression of its constructive coordinates revealed that the cross sections of this structural typology are entirely constituted by third-degree polynomials, with an R^2 factor higher than 98% in all instances analyzed. Their parametric modeling also demonstrated that the curves of these cross-sections are not sine waves (sinusoids).

TABLE 02: **List of polynomials resulting from the polynomial regression of the case study sections.**

Case Study	*Polynomial corresponding to the key cross section*	*R^2 factor*	*Polynomial corresponding to the key longitudinal section*	*R^2 factor*
Caputto Factory	$y = -0.0631x^3 + 0.5707x^2 - 0.8989x + 0.3813$	0.9993	$y = -0.0087x^2 - 4E\text{-}05x + 4.1849$	1
Port Warehouse	$y = -0.0743x^3 + 0.5707x^2 - 0.8989x + 0.3826$	0.998	$y = -0.0086x^2 + \text{-}05x + 4.3075$	0.998
Ferrando Warehouse	$y = -0.0962x^3 + 0.5707x^2 - 0.8989x + 0.3114$	0.9996	$y = -0.0128x^2\ 0,0015x + 2.3824$	1
Tobacco Factory	$y = -0.0584x^3 + 0.5707x^2 - 0.8989x + 0.3444$	0.9983	$y = -0.0097x^2\ 0,0005x + 3.5992$	0.9999
Hermanos Maristas School	$y = -0.0602x^3 + 0.5707x^2 - 0.8989x + 0.1315$	0.9995	$y = -0.0175x^2\ 0,0013x + 1.8111$	1
Palenga Warehouse	$y = -0.054x^3 + 0.5707x^2 - 0.8989x + 0.3643$	0.9992	$y = -0.0099x^2\ 0,0006x + 3.5043$	1
Cine Cel Cur	$y = -0.0675x^3 + 0.5707x^2 - 0.8989x + 0.1421$	0.999	$y = -0.0211x^2\ 0,0089x + 2.5914$	0.997
Frai Marcos Warehouse	$y = -0.057x^3 + 0.5707x^2 - 0.8989x + 0.1465$	0.9994	$y = -0.0236x^2\ 0,0059x + 3.2349$	1
La Piedras Altas Warehouse	$y = -0.0784x^3 + 0.5707x^2 - 0.8989x + 0.1768$	0.9981	$y = -0.0145x^2\ 0,0015x + 5.5387$	1

Source: MELACHOS, Felipe Corres. 1 table. 2019

The polynomial regression of all cross sections in *R* software (Figure 8) indicated the existence of a 3rd degree polynomial capable of synthesizing their geometry: $\boldsymbol{Y = -0.040052.\ X^3 + 0.357741.\ X^2 - 0.41699.\ X + 0.186390.}$

This polynomial showed an R^2 factor higher than 93%, attesting to its reliability. However, the same analysis indicated that the R2 factor fell to only 44% at the highest point of the section, indicating a significant variation in this portion of the curve. In the cross sections, the result was a 2nd-degree polynomial, but with a degree of reliability below 40%.

FIGURE 8: **Polynomial regression of the cross and longitudinal sections of all case studies in software *R*.**

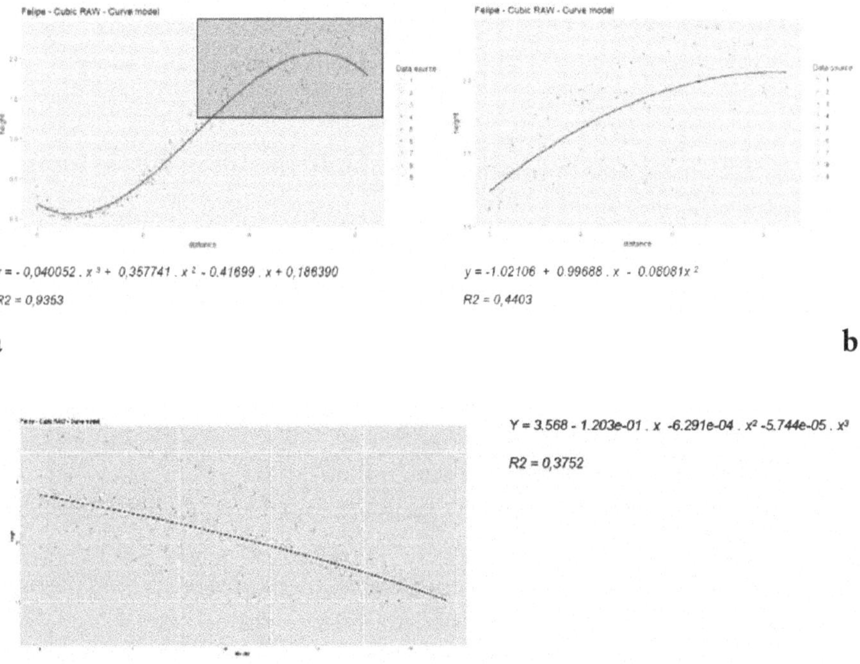

Figure 8. (a) Polynomial regression of the key cross sections in *R*, and resulting high-reliability 3rd-degree polynomial, with a region of greater dispersion of points highlighted in red and enlarged (b), where we were able to obtain a resulting low-reliability 2nd-degree polynomial. Polynomial regression of the longitudinal section in the *R*, with a resulting low-reliability 2nd-degree polynomial.
Source: MELACHOS, Felipe Corres. 2 models. 2019

The same procedure of longitudinal sections indicated that the geometry of their curves consists of 2nd-degree polynomials in all analyzed instances, with an R^2 factor of reliability higher than 99% in the case studies. The redrawing of longitudinal sections indicated that their spans are not uniform and range from 20.40 meters to 50.00 meters in size.

This same procedure revealed that their sags are variable and directly proportional to the transverse span, usually staying in the ratio of 1 to 10 to its span. For longitudinal sections, larger spans did not necessarily imply larger transverse spans.

Regarding the surfaces of the Gaussian vaults of the case studies, the Gaussian analyzes performed using parametric modeling (Tab. 3) indicated that the structural modules of this typology are divided into three surface classifications:

1 – Anticlastic and approximately folding surfaces, with hyperbolic geometric matrix;

2 – Folding surfaces, with parabolic geometric matrix;

3 – Synclastic surfaces, approximately foldable, of an elliptical geometric matrix.

The approximation shown in Table 3.b demonstrates how most of the surface areas of the discontinuous Gaussian vault structural modules are at a zero *k* (Gaussian curvature measurement index), indicated in green. This suggests that most of their surfaces are foldable and with a parabolic geometric matrix. However, as there are other *k* values on their surfaces, these structures can be classified as approximately foldable freeform surfaces as *their* k values in the other regions are almost zero.

The parametric modeling for Gaussian analysis of these surfaces, together with their design, did not indicate relations between *k* values and their longitudinal and transverse spans. Nor were there any relations between *k* values and the sag and span proportions of the structural modules.

When analyzing the chosen Gaussian vaults' minimum curvature, both in Table 3.a and in the approximation of Table 3.b, we verify a predominance of blue areas. These blue areas indicate mean h curvatures of value 0, which indicates areas of minimal surface. The other surface areas analyzed are very close to, but they do not reach 0, and we can state that the surfaces of the discontinuous Gaussian vaults analyzed are *almost minimal.* This analysis also rejects the possibility of this typology being friendly to construction in pneumatic variables since its average curvature is not constant.

Table 03: Analysis of curvature of the surfaces of the case studies.

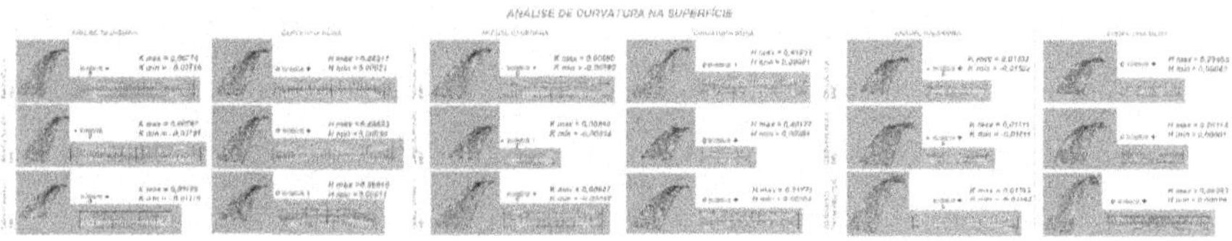

a

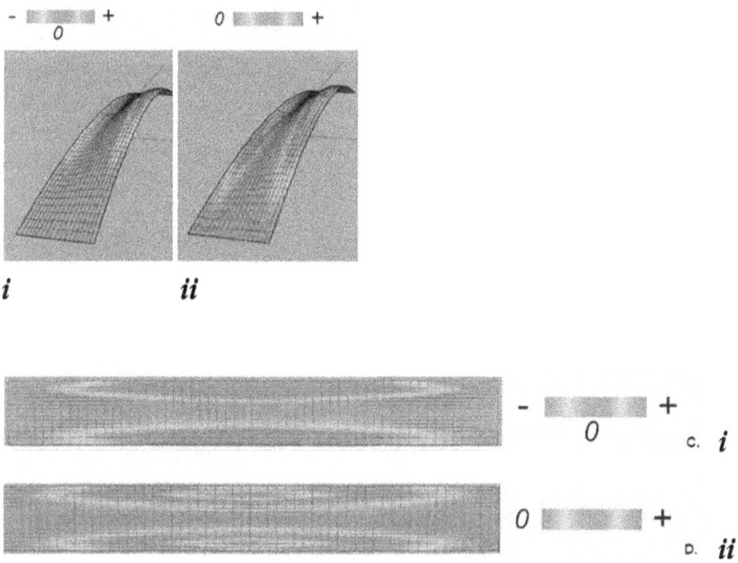

b

(Tab. 3.a) Parametric analysis of Gaussian curvature *k* and mean curvature *h* of all case studies; (Tab. 3.b) Detail of the *k* (*i*) and *h* (*ii*) values.
Source: (Tab. 3.a) MELACHOS, Felipe Corres. 1 table. 2019; (Tab. 3.b) MELACHOS, Felipe Corres. 2 models. 2019.

Finally, we performed analyzes of the quality of the space generated by the discontinuous Gaussian vaults using the Brazilian illuminance indexes applied to natural light. Table 4 indicates that this structural solution implies variable visual comfort rates so that the spaces resulting from their geometry are impossible to be used for professional purposes without the support of artificial light.

TABLE 4: **Parametric analysis of illuminance.**

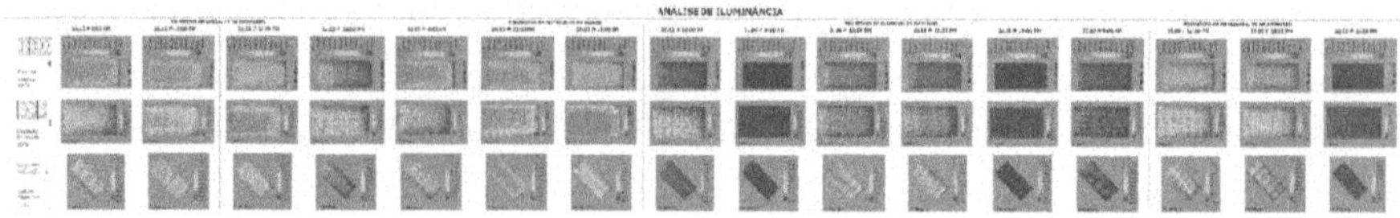

a

b

c

(Tab. 4.a) Illuminance analysis through parametric modeling of the first 3 case studies: Caputto Factory, Port Warehouse, and Ferrando Factory. (Tab. 4.b) Detail of the illuminance analysis for the Port Warehouse. (Tab. 4.c) Interiors of the Montevideo Port Warehouse lit by natural light.

Source: (Tab. 4.a; 4.b) MELACHOS, Felipe Corres. 2 tables. 2019; (Tab. 4.c) FINOTTI, Leonardo. 1 photo. 2011.

Four of the case studies analyzed (Hermanos Maristas School Gymnasium, Cin Cel Cur Factory, Frai Marcos Factory, Las Piedras Altas Warehouse, and Factory) showed most of the measurements below the borderline index of 200 lux. On the other hand, three of the case studies (Port Warehouse, Tobacco Factory, and Palenga Warehouse) presented most of the measurements with indexes partially above 200 lux.

Only the Caputto Factory and the Ferrando Factory showed illuminance indexes above 200 lux, allowing their use for professional purposes without the support of artificial lighting. The metrics used for measurement in this portion of the analysis of the results are based on ABNT NBR ISO/CIE 8995-1:2013.

Discussion

The main objective of this last section of the chapter is to interpret the results obtained during the research compared to the state-of-the-art of the study theme, aiming at demonstrating the proof of the central hypothesis of the doctoral thesis. Therefore, as occurred when establishing the results obtained and their analysis, this section will be developed along the topics "section," "surface," and "illuminance."

The results obtained regarding the sections of the discontinuous Gaussian vaults designed and built by Eladio Dieste prove the hypothesis that there is a set of underlying geometric relationships in their constitution, going well beyond a mere geometric similarity. In fact, this thesis has proven that the cross sections of this structural typology are constituted essentially by 3rd-degree polynomials and not sine waves (sinusoids), as pointed out by Martin Bechthold (2008).

The lack of knowledge about this typology was such that Stanford Anderson (2004), one of the authors of the most established anthologies about Eladio Dieste, defined the cross section of his continuous vaults as "S." Some authors such as Ochsendorf (2004) have described their geometry, but not in a concrete definition: "If, however, the catenary sag gradually varies as it moves, then we have a wavy surface. The waves are more pronounced in the center of the catenary and diminish [as they move away from the center] until they are completely flat at the starting points. (OCHSENDORF, p. 144, translation by the authors)." This research, on the other hand, has reached an equation capable of synthesizing the curvature of these hitherto unexplored sections through the 3rd degree polynomial below:

$$y = -0.040052.X^3 + 0.357741.X^2 - 0.41699.X + 0.186390.$$

Understanding the longitudinal section of the discontinuous Gaussian vaults was already known through another geometric representation – that of the catenary. This notion is present in the writings of Dieste himself in Carbonell (1987), in the anthology written by Torrecillas and Pérez (1996), Anderson (2004), Bechthold (2008), and Ochsendorf (2004).

In the context of the cross sections, the hypothesis is confirmed mainly by the demonstration that it is constituted by second-degree polynomials. This demonstration is an original contribution made by this research.

The logic of catenary persists in attempts to demonstrate understanding of the surfaces generated by the discontinuous Gaussian vaults: *"We chose the catenary as a guideline, then the weight produces simple compression; and this compression makes the structure capable of resisting bending."* (DIESTE *in* TORRECILLAS, PÉREZ, 1996, p. 41)." Allen (2004) classifies them as "cylindrical" surfaces, whereas Anderson (2004) emphasizes their tridimensionality and undulations, with aiming at controlling their rigidity.

Pedreschi and Larrambebere (2004) highlight their undulations, in addition to the aspect of the catenary and their gradually variable sag – a remarkable attempt to understand their double-curvature. However, notwithstanding the above, this research defines the geometry of these surfaces as being:

> [...] consisting of a corrugated shell, composed of horizontally translated catenary sections, but with a gradually variable sag, which may have its undulations interrupted or not by openings: the discontinuous or continuous Gaussian vaults.
>
> [...] numerically freeform surface[s], but approximately foldable
>
> [...] *almost minimal.* (MELACHOS, 2020, p. 307, emphasis by the author).

Therefore, the proof of the hypothesis also extends to the surface of these structural typologies, emphasizing its structural efficiency and geometric adaptation for contemporary production by digital means through its predominance as a foldable surface. The methodology for proving this hypothesis also constitutes an original contribution of this research, given the scarcity of parametric analyses about Eladio Dieste's work.

Another significant contribution of this research is the understanding and taxonomy of the typologies produced by Eladio Dieste, since only Dieste made the distinction between continuous and discontinuous Gaussian vaults, but discreetly (CARBONELL, 1987; TORRECILLAS, PÉREZ, 1996). Unfortunately, this distinction was ignored by some authors such as Pedreschi and Larrambebere (2004) and Bechthold (2008). Still, this research rescued the original taxonomy attributed by Dieste himself in the analysis of his own work.

Finally, the research conducted approaches an unprecedented parametric analysis aiming at the quality of space conformed by the discontinuous Gaussian vaults, one of the main suggestions made in the thesis qualification exam. The findings of this research demonstrate that these spaces do not function only using natural lighting, contrary to what was affirmed by Dieste in (CARBONELL, 1987; TORRECILLAS, PÉREZ, 1996). Anderson (2004) and Maria Cristina Ramos de Carvalho's thesis (2004), one of the best works about the constructive technique of reinforced ceramics in Portuguese, point only to the entry of natural lighting, but not to the measuring of the quality of this light.

However, rather than seeking innovations, this work aimed to demonstrate to the rest of the planet the presence of great *structural artists* (MELACHOS; FLORIO, 2018) in the Latin American continent and promote the preservation of modern heritage in the continent. Therefore, the work of Eladio Dieste deserves to be disseminated around the globe and presents a tremendous didactic potential for our students to study formal-structural conceptions and constructive techniques that go beyond the materials considered "traditional," which hardly ever offer satisfactory performance considering our social context and climate-geographic conditions.

The training received abroad through the PDSE-CAPES program at the Università degli Studi di Ferrara was very important for developing this work, providing technological inputs and additional primary and secondary sources that greatly enriched the research. More importantly, this period spent abroad allowed the participants of the research to come in contact with professional academic research structures abroad, import knowledge about innovative digital design tools into undergraduate and graduate education in national higher education institutions, and obtain a valuable collection of good practices to promote academic research and production.

By coincidence, it was precisely in this European institution where Nicholas Copernicus studied, and his mathematical precepts transformed astronomy for all and forever. If Copernicus sensed that the earth revolves around the sun, Dieste sensed that the construction of the maximum from the very minimum starts with respect for its local constraints.

Bibliographical References

ALLEN, E. *Guastavino, Dieste, and the two Revolutions in Masonry Vaulting*. In: ANDERSON, S. (org.). ***Eladio Dieste: Innovation in Structural Art***. New York, Princeton Architectural Press, 2004.

ANDERSON, S. (org.). ***Eladio Dieste: Innovation in Structural Art***. New York, Princeton Architectural Press, 2004.

ABNT – Brazilian Association of Technical Standards/*Associação Brasileira de Normas Técnicas*. ***NBR 5413: Working environment lighting – Part 1***. Rio de Janeiro. 2013.

BECHTHOLD, M. ***Innovative Surface Structures – Technologies and Applications***. New York: Taylor & Francis, 2008.

BONTA, Juan Pablo. ***Eladio Dieste***. Buenos Aires, 1963.

CARBONELL, G. (org.). ***Eladio Dieste – La Estructura Ceramica***. Escala: 1987.

CARVALHO, M. C. R. ***Caracterização da Tecnologia Construtiva de Eladio Dieste: Contribuições para a Inovação do Projeto Arquitetônico e da Construção em Alvenaria Estrutural***. Thesis (PhD in Architecture and Urbanism). Department of Civil Engineering, UFSC, Universidade Federal de Santa Catarina, Florianópolis, 2004.

DIESTE, Eladio. *Bóvedas gausas*. In: TORRECILLAS, Antonio Jiménez; PÉREZ, Martin de Porres Ramírez. **Eladio Dieste 1943-1966**. Sevilla: Junta de Andalucia, 1996, V.1. p. 41-85.

DIESTE, E. *La cerámica armada*. In: CARBONELL, G. **Eladio Dieste – La Estructura Cerámica**. Escala: 1987.

FLORIO, W. *Modelagem Paramétrica em Arquitetura: Estratégias para materializar Formas Complexas*. In: **SIGraDi 2009**. Proceedings of the 13th Congress of the Iberoamerican Society of Digital Graphics, Graphics, São Paulo, Brazil.

MENDENHALL, W; BEAVER, R.; and BEAVER, B. ***Introduction to Probability and Statistics***. Belmont: Duxbury, 2006.

MELACHOS, Felipe Corres. ***Análise Paramétrica das Abóbodas Gaussianas de Eladio Dieste.*** Thesis (PhD in Architecture and Urbanism), Post-Graduate Program in Architecture and Urbanism, Universidade Presbiteriana Mackenzie & Dipartamento de Architettura, Università degli Studi di Ferrara, São Paulo and Ferrara, 2020.

MELACHOS, F. C. ; FLORIO, W. *Eladio Dieste, un artista strutturale dell'America latina – Contributi originali sul processo di progettazione delle superfici strutturali.* **Paesaggio Urbano**, v.1, p.110 – 121, 2018.

OCHSENDORF, J. A. *Eladio Dieste as Structural Artist.* In: ANDERSON, S. (Org.). **Eladio Dieste: Innovation in Structural Art.** New York, Princeton Architectural Press, 2004. p. 94-105.

PEDRESCHI, R., LARRAMBEBERE, G. *Technology and Innovation in the work of Eladio Dieste.* In: STANFORD, Anderson. ***Eladio Dieste: Innovation in Structural Art.*** New York, Princeton Architectural Press, 2004.

TORECILLAS, A. J.; PEREZ, M. P. R. (org.). **Eladio Dieste 1943-1996**. Sevilla: Junta de Andalucia, 1996. V. 1.

________. **Eladio Dieste 1943-1996 –** ***Métodos de Cálculo / Calculation Methods.*** Sevilla: Junta de Andalucia, 1996. V. 2.

UNESCO. *La obra del ingeniero Eladio Dieste en Uruguay.* **Para la Prensa**. 2014. Available at: <http://www.unesco.org/new/es/media-services/single-view-tvrelease/news/the_work_of_the_engineer_eladio_Dieste_in_uruguay//>. Accessed on October 31, 2021.

UNESCO. *The work of engineer Eladio Dieste: Church of Atlántida.* **World Heritage List.** 2021. Available at: < https://whc.unesco.org/en/list/1612/>. Accessed on: October 31, 2021.

3. URBAN SPACE, SOCIAL EXCLUSION, AND "JURIDICITY REGIMES": AN APPROACH BASED ON ÉTIENNE LE ROY'S "THEORY OF MULTIJURIDISM"

Orlando Villas Bôas Filho
Matteo Finco

Introduction

Several authors emphasize that urban social exclusion and "dispossession of rights" submit those involved to new regulation dynamics. Faria (2002, p. 120), for example, alludes to the existence of a *marginal law*, consisting of a "self-produced normativity in fourth-world ghettos" that, in his view, renders the monopolistic claim to the regulation of a positive state law and formal courts problematic.[1] Resorting to his empirical studies carried out in Brazil, Portugal, and Cape Verde, Santos (2002a, p. 205) emphasizes that "not one, but several forms of law or modes of juridicity circulate in society. The official, state law, which is in the codes and is legislated by the government or parliament, is just one of these forms, although it tends to be the most important one."[2] Rouland (2003), referring to "hidden rights"

[1] According to Faria (2002, p. 120), the contemporary legal regulation is fragmented, among other things, due to the existence of a "self-produced normativity in fourth-world ghettos, such as the one currently in force in the hills of Rio de Janeiro and in the huge slums of São Paulo and other large Brazilian cities, in the miserable belts of Mexico City, Bogotá, and Lima, in the degraded outskirts of Caracas, Buenos Aires, and Johannesburg, in the ethnic neighborhoods of Los Angeles, London, Brussels, Paris, Berlin, and Hamburg [...]." On "marginal law," see also: Faria (2010).

[2] In the midst of his "symbolic cartography of law," Santos (2002a, p. 206) underlines "the existence of local rights in rural areas, in marginal urban neighborhoods, in churches, companies, sports, and in professional organizations."

(*droits caches*), identifies, among them, the "popular rights" produced in the context of modernity and widely spread in Western societies, both in urban and rural areas.[3]

Obviously, it is not a question of limiting these forms of informal regulation or non-state legality to contexts of social exclusion.[4] However, it is a fact that "regimes of juridicity" circulate within them, being understood as an expression of different forms of implementation of legal regulation distinct from state law.[5] The "theory of multijuridism"[6] proposed by Étienne Le Roy is particularly appropriate for a socio-legal approach to this issue, as it conveys a complex conception of legal regulations that decentralizes it from its state form of expression.[7] Thus, we will first briefly address the issue of exclusion and socioeconomic and civil vulnerability in the urban space of contemporary Brazil (I). We will then focus on a few aspects of Étienne Le Roy's (II) "theory of multijuridism," and, finally, bring it to bear as an analytical instrument for "decoding" the "regimes of juridicity" in the context of social exclusion in the Brazilian urban space (III).

[3] Rouland (2003, p. 186-187) asserts that "popular rights (they also exist in our societies) occupy an extensive area, at least as large as state law, but one that is difficult to explore due to its unofficial nature. The highest category of legal pluralism, they are formed outside state instances, both in urban and rural areas. They also quite often break away from traditional rights and from the solutions inherited from the past, as they are essentially innovative."

[4] Regarding this issue, Carvalho (2009, p. 215), referring to the Brazilian social stratification, states that "first-class citizens" are favored; those "who are above the law, who always manage to defend their interests through the power of money and of social prestige. [...] They often have important ties to businesses, government, and the Judiciary itself. These ties allow the law to only work to their benefit."

[5] For a definition of the notion of "regimes of juridicity" in the sense in which it is used here, see: Villas Bôas Filho (2014).

[6] It is worth noting that we write the expression "theory of multijuridism" in inverted commas because this is the way used by Étienne Le Roy's interlocutors, such as Eberhard (2001 and 2010). Le Roy (1998 and 1999) uses the expression "hypothèse du multijuridisme" or simply "multijuridisme."

[7] For an analysis of the importance and challenges of socio-legal research, see, for example: Arnaud (1988 and 1992), Bailleux and Ost (2013), Dumont and Bailleux (2010), and Villas Bôas Filho (2018a, 2018b, and 2019).

1. Exclusion and socioeconomic and civil vulnerability: The degradation of citizenship in the urban space of contemporary Brazil

In his expressive analysis of the "Brazilian social issue," Kowarick (2002) points to "de-citizenization" as a process engendered by socioeconomic and civil vulnerability in urban Brazil.[8] The author starts from the premise that, during the 1980s and 1990s, a democratic political system was consolidated in the country (at least formally)[9], without, however, civil and social rights having been established. This resulted in a vulnerability of the population (especially the low-income one) with respect of basic rights, due to public systems of protection that have always been chronically precarious and that, moreover, have been dismantled in recent years, making them even less effective and inclusive. In this context, where social exclusion is rampant, citizenship becomes extremely problematic, leading to an obvious overload on the Brazilian state law's capacity to respond to demands that are structurally beyond its reach.

Therefore, as emphasized by Kowarick (2002 and 2009), what could be called the "Brazilian social issue" refers, above all, to the deficit in the expansion of citizenship rights.[10] Thus, referring to the "Brazilian social issue," Kowarick (2002 and 2009) uses, although he problematizes them, the concepts of "disaffiliation," "vulnerability," and "exclusion" developed

[8] Similarly, Kowarick (2009, p. 102), without alluding to the notion of "de-citizenization," emphasizes that, "in our cities' current scenario, *massive socioeconomic and civil vulnerability processes* are underway." Of course, this is exacerbated in the context of the COVID-19 pandemic.

[9] For a critique of the reduction of the democratic experience only to its electoral--representative dimension, see: Rosanvallon (2008).

[10] In this regard, Kowarick (2002, p. 16) makes the following consideration: "What is our social issue? There are several, but the one that stands out the most in the sphere of the relations between State and society perhaps resides in the difficulty of expanding citizenship rights. After a decade of struggles and demands, in a context in which a democratic political system is gradually consolidated, there is no longer an organizational and claiming aggregations to consolidate a set of basic rights. They may appear in the 1988 Charter, but are not translated into the strengthening of an institutional field of negotiation of conflicts and arbitration, nor into broad social policies." In that same regard, and complementing this assertion, Kowarick (2009, p. 77) states that "there were no processes that led to the consideration of a condition of empowerment of groups and categories of civil society." Therefore, it could be stated that, in the perspective of Rosanvallon (2008) there is a commitment to democratic legitimacy, especially in its "proximity" dimension.

by Castel (1991, 1995, and 2003[1995]).[11] It is worth noting, however, that we are dealing with issues that find their causes in the present, and not in remnants of a past whose perennial effects seem to remain unchanged. It is evident that the fact that Brazil was a slave society until the late 19th century, and that it developed a "structural rabble"[12] which, although free, was historically excluded from the basic productive dynamics of the Colony, the Empire, and, later, of the new social an economic order, causes a resurgence of the pernicious effects that permeate its "social issue,"[13] making even more dramatic both the situation and the inability to solve issues related to a citizenship that formally gets rhetorical support in the Constitution, but which suffers from a chronic deficit of implementation.

Thus, when addressing the themes of "vulnerability," "disaffiliation," and "exclusion," by indicating their specificities in the Brazilian society, Kowarick (2002 and 2009) emphasizes that he does not intend to return to the issues related to our "curse of origin," or to the culturalist analyses concerning the permanence of the "Brazilian *ethos*" as an explanatory category of our illness, since, according to him, the verification of patrimonial- and paternalistic-style commitments – the favor and the gift – in urban-capitalist Brazil refers to a complex, diverse, and always renewed combination, and not to a set of essences that survived from a remote past, impregnated in our roots.

Just as Robert Castel analyzes the effects of *disaffiliation* based on the consequences engendered by modernity itself, in which a wage-earning society develops,[14] Kowarick (2002, p. 22) also seeks to indicate the issues

[11] Although he emphasizes that unlike the French case, in the Brazilian one is not possible to see the weakening of rights as a crisis of the wage-earning society, Kowarick (2003 and 2009) structures his analysis based on the concepts developed by Castel (1991 and 2003[1995]).

[12] When analyzing the process of peripheral modernization, Souza (2003) points to the establishment of a "structural rabble," deprived of rights.

[13] The very use of the expression "social issue" already indicates that Kowarick's analysis (2002 and 2009) refers to modernity. Referring to the expression "social issue," Rosanvallon (1995, p. 7) pointed out that ""cette expression, lancée à la fin du XIXe siècle, renvoyait aux dysfonctionnements de la société industrielle naissante."

[14] Castel (1991 and 2003[1995]) emphasizes this aspect, comparing the issue of exclusion in the modern wage-earning society to exclusion in pre-modern times. Referring to the French context, Castel (2003[1995], p. 14) locates "dans les années 1960 la matrice de base de la 'société salariale' moderne." However, Kowarick (2009, p. 77) asserts that, in the Brazilian case, "the weakening of rights cannot be seen as a result of the crisis of the wage society [...].

of vulnerability and exclusion in the context of modern urban Brazil, conceiving them, ultimately, as indicative of a situation of "dispossession of rights" that, at the limit, leads to the condition that Hannah Arendt attributes to outcasts and the stateless: the absence of the "right to have rights."[15] This situation that produces a "confined," "third-class," or even "non-existent" citizenship, despite being accentuated due to the systematic exclusion that occurs in our historical-social formation, does not derive entirely from it.[16] It is important to note that this form of exclusion is produced and even accentuated by the dynamics of modernity itself.[17] That is why Kowarick (2002, p. 30) asserts that his intention is to emphasize "that in our cities' current scenario, broad socioeconomic and civil vulnerability processes are underway, leading to what can be called a process of de-citizenization" (2002, p. 30)."[18]

The reason for this is because, in the strong sense of the term, there has never been such a modality in Brazil, nor in Latin America [...]."

[15] Kowarick (2009, p. 89) states that "it is clear that it is possible to speak of social separation when considering the abysmal differences that separate strata of our pointed social pyramid." Hannah Arendt describes the right to have rights as the right "to live in a framework where one is judged by one's actions and opinions," in other words, "to belong to some kind of organized community" (ARENDT, 1966 [1951], p. 177).

[16] When focusing on citizenship in Brazil, Carvalho (2009, p. 216) says there are three classes, and, in his understanding, the third of them, which comprises the "marginal population of large cities, urban and rural workers without a formal contract, squatters, maids, people doing odd jobs, street vendors, abandoned minors, and beggars," does not feel protected by formal law.

[17] In an analysis that contrasts France, United States, and Latin America, Didier Fassin emphasizes the modern character of the phenomena that, in these countries, are called, respectively, *exclusion*, *underclass*, and *marginalidad*. According to Fassin (1996, p. 37), "la décennie quatre-vingts a été marquée, en de nombreux endroits du monde, par une aggravation des inégalités sociales et par l'apparition de ce que l'on parfois appelé 'la nouvelle pauvreté'." One should also keep in mind that the critical reflection on modernity, even from different perspectives, has underlined the need to reconsider traditional categories and views of the modernization process (Appadurai, 2014; Harvey, 2015; Touraine, 2019; Santos, 2018). However, the myth of the modern city seems to resist as an archetype based on which the development of metropolises is measured at a global level. This legitimizes and feeds the "production" of the excluded, under-included, and of the marginalized.

[18] In this sense, Kowarick's perspective (2002 and 2009) is in line with the following statement made by Castel (2003[1995], p. 15): "c'est de l'histoire du présent qu'il s'agit."

In fact, it seems appropriate to refer to Santos' criticism of the so-called "sluggish reason" of Eurocentric rationality – which mortifies the present in favor of an idea of a future under the banner of civilization and progress, and which considers the universal and the global to the detriment of the local. Indicating two types of sociability, in the sense of the predominant forms assumed by social relations in a given historical and geographical context, Santos defines "metropolitan" and "colonial" sociability. While the former is the Western civilization's traditional type, the latter – typical of "Southern" world contexts – is more recent, and is regulated by the tension between appropriation (assimilation, etc.) and violence. Since it is the type of sociability that determines social inclusion and exclusion, the disregard of colonial sociability and its forms implies the non-recognition of the perspective of the "non-citizens," of the marginalized and, therefore, predictably, also of alternative forms of law to the traditional Western one (Santos, 2002b and 2014; Ricotta, 2019).

The production of exclusion is, therefore, particularly striking in contexts of great inequalities such as that of contemporary Brazil. It is not by chance that a sociologist like Niklas Luhmann defines "favelas" as places where the meaninglessness of talking about exploitation is even more evident: what could "capital" enjoy in such contexts, where individuals, reduced to *bodies*, lose the dimension of *people*, in the sense of "actors" able to "participate" in society and its different functionally specialized spheres (Economy, Education, Law, etc.)? (LUHMANN, 1998).

In fact, Luhmann (1998) points out that also in contexts that could be defined as "marginal" – and this is also true in the West, for example in Southern Italy[19] – forms of sociability different from the traditional Western ones develop. For example, giving more importance to perception of dangers and violence (LUHMANN, 2005, p. 42-43). Therefore, if it is true that there is an incessant production of exclusion, a "delocalized, floating, dematerialized production of otherness" (DE GIORGI, 2017, p. 44), in the same "peripheries" of modernity, there is also the production of "resistance" to the typically modern and Western rationality of the differentiation of society, with individuals becoming more dependent on each other (De Giorgi, 2006, p. 22). These different forms of sociability are basically what De Giorgi (1998) calls "inclusion networks".

[19] On this issue, see also: Corsi; De Giorgi, 1998; Corsi, 1998.

2. Étienne Le Roy's "theory of multijuridism"

Inspired by the notion of "interlegality" proposed by Boaventura de Sousa Santos, Le Roy (1998) develops the idea of "multijuridism" as a way of apprehending the modes of social regulation that, by virtue of their imposition, acquire a legal status. It is a perspective that, in line with the theories of legal pluralism, intends to take on the complexity of legal regulation to reject the monistic and formalist representation that reduces the complexity to the norms established and applied by the State.[20] However, multijuridism intends to advance in relation to the theories of legal pluralism being that it moves away from the "unitary archetype" that, according to Le Roy (1998), characterizes them.[21] In this perspective, Le Roy (1999 and 2017) proposes to differentiate "law" (*droit*) and "juridicity" (*juridicité*).[22]

Based on this distinction, law is seen as a specific regulatory mechanism, historically developed by modern Western societies, within a broader legality that encompasses it.[23] Thus, the term juridicity, as conceptualized by Le Roy (1998, 1999 and 2017), presents a unique ability to explain the ethnocentrism that permeates our analytical experience in relation to law and that entails a concealment of other "landscapes"[24] of juridicity by virtue of the supposed universality of the Western one. According to the French author, modern Western law is nothing more than an "avatar"

[20] To Le Roy (1998, p. 38), "le multijuridisme, qui intègre le multiple dans l'idée juridique, doit être abordé non comme un ensemble statique d'injonctions ou de sanctions, mais comme un système ouvert, dynamique, comme un jeu ou comme un processus dont on doit reformuler les règles par un nouveau paradigme." It should be noted that Blankertz and Goodman (1980, p. 34) too support the argumentation that to have rights is not essential a State. They conceived law as constituted by customs, contracts, and statutes established among social groups and, within them, among the people who are part of them.

[21] We cannot build upon this issue here. It must be emphasized, however, that Le Roy (1998, p. 34), based on Michel Alliot, states that those who defend legal pluralism "récusent le monopole juridique exercé par l'État tout en restant prisonniers de l'archétype unitaire, version moderne du monothéisme: UN Dieu, UN État, Un Droit."

[22] In this regard, see: Eberhard (2001 and 2010) and Villas Bôas Filho (2014, 2015 and 2017).

[23] As emphasized Le Roy (2017, p. 29), "[le] droit est ainsi une application particulière d'un phénomène plus général, la juridicité."

[24] The term "landscapes" appears here in the sense originally proposed by Arjun Appadurai, and indicates the plurality of imaginary worlds historically situated in the global context. Étienne Le Roy (2011b) is inspired by Appadurai to propose the notion of *ethoscape*.

of the juridicity that includes and transcends it. Therefore, if the law expresses only a specific form of historical and cultural concretion of a broader phenomenon, a universal dimension should not be attributed to it. According to Le Roy (2004; 2007; 2009; 2011a; 2011b; 2011c, and 2017), this tendency to attribute universality to a particular form of expression of a broader phenomenon implies a form of ethnocentrism, as there are other means of social regulation and conceptions of the "legal phenomenon" different from the Western one but equally legitimate.

This approach, refuting the conventional representation of law, also challenges the traditional conceptions about the sociology of law (its definition, function, objectives, etc.) and, consequently, the conceptions concerning the relations between law and society. However, it is worth noting that, within the scope of the sociology of law, there has always been a broad debate about the expansion of the concept of law beyond its traditional Western-state form. In this sense, it suffices to think of Eugen Ehrlich's classic work on "living law" (*lebende Recht*)[25]

Le Roy (1998, 1999 and 2017) asserts that "law" consists of a *folk system* which, as a set of norms sanctioned by the State, constitutes only a particular form of experience, proper to a historical and social context – the modern West – which, for this reason, could not be generalized as universal.[26] However, despite this, nothing is more common among jurists than the assertion of the supposed universality of law, through the projection for all societies of the characteristics it takes on in the Western tradition. In addition, under the influence of a recurring monistic view, the "legal phenomenon" tends to be considered from the perspective of its positivization, that is, inexorably tied to the State.[27]

[25] Regarding this, see, among others: Febbrajo (2010; 2013) and Ferrari (2010).

[26] Le Roy (2004, p. 426) stresses that "la définition occidentale du Droit comme ensemble de normes sanctionnées par l'État ne correspond qu'à un *folk system*, un type d'expérience particulier, propre à un moment de l'histoire qui ne peut ni être généralisé (tant les divergences sont profondes entre traditions juridiques) ni sans doute généralisable (le présupposé évolutionniste qui le sous-tend étant illusoire)."

[27] It should be noted that alluding to the positivization of law as its essential characteristic in the historical experience of the modern West does not imply reducing it to its state dimension of expression. In any case, as Bourdieu (1993, 1994, and 2012) emphasizes, given the centrality assumed by the State as an institution claiming the monopoly of legitimate physical and symbolic violence, in the reproduction and canonization of forms of social

Thus, first of all, it should be noted that juridicity, as conceived by Le Roy (1999, 2013, and 2017), is on a different level than law. Therefore, its scope is much broader and includes positive law, which, in this perspective, is conceived as an expression of one of the possible forms of the historical and cultural concretion of a broader phenomenon of social regulation that can be characterized as legal by virtue of its mandatory and, therefore, sanctionable nature: Juridicity.[28] Thus, since the notion of juridicity refers to the set of cultural configurations on a broader scale, it allows to analyze the "legal phenomenon" detaching from a conception centered on positive law.[29]

A second important aspect that should be noted about Le Roy's (1999, 2011c, and 2017) perspective on juridicity is that it implies the obligatory character of an act or a relationship, that is, the possibility of imposing a sanction (*sanctionnabilité*)[30], no matter the guarantor authority, as long as it is capable of apply it. This means that there are different types of sanctions that rest on different and complementary fundamentals and, consequently, that the State is not the only institution with the authority to sanction. According to the author, this implies a clear legal pluralism.[31] In fact, Le Roy (2004; 2011c; 2013) underlines that sanctions, as an expression of the recognition of the mandatory nature of regulation, whatever the authority that institutes them, consist of the diacritical trait that law and juridicity have in common. Thus, everything defined as legal is sanctioned. However, as emphasized by Le Roy (2011a), sanctions should not be conceived here as a synonym of punishment, but simply as an expression of recognition,

classification, this association between law and state becomes natural. In this regard, see: Villas Bôas Filho (2021).

[28] Le Roy (2015, p. 200) emphasizes the need to "repenser le rapport juridique dans le cadre d'une théorie 'transmoderne' de la juridicité intégrant ce que les Occidentaux dénomment 'le droit' et les autres le 'li et le fa' en Chine, le 'dharma' en Inde, la coutume en Afrique, les usages locaux ou la pratique des affaires chez nous."

[29] In this regard, worthy of note is the proposal made by Boaventura de Sousa Santos which, although based on different assumptions, has significant parallels with that of Étienne Le Roy. In fact, as seen above, Le Roy (1998) analyzes the parallels between his notion of multijuridism and that of interlegality proposed by Boaventura de Sousa Santos.

[30] As analyzed below, from Le Roy's perspective (1999 and 2011c), sanctions consist of the diacritical feature common to law and juridicity.

[31] In any case, it is worth noting that Le Roy (1998, 2003, and 2017) specifies his position on the discussion on legal pluralism. On this issue, see: Villas Bôas Filho (2014).

based on different procedures, of the mandatory nature of the devices employed in the regulation.

A third aspect to be highlighted about juridicity is that it corresponds to the characteristic of social practices to be able to respond to a purpose through coercive imposition. Therefore, relying on Pierre Legendre, Le Roy (1998, 1999; 2004; 2011a, and 2017) highlights the role it plays in reproducing life in society. Therefore, juridicity is not an undisputed space. Le Roy (2009) asserts that it is a force field characterized by the tensions inherent to social life and in which there is pressure to obtain solutions to conflicts. However, when discussed conceptually, juridicity rises to the level of "concept rector" (*concept-recteur*) of a "dynamic anthropology of social regulations" (LE ROY, 2011b, p. 18).

It should be noted that Le Roy (2011b, 2011c, and 2017) asserts the complementarity relationship between "law" and "juridicity." By doing so, he emphasizes that his intention is not to devalue an experience – expressed in "law" – in favor of another, which is that of "juridicity." It is simply a matter of problematizing the identification of the "legal phenomenon" with the law, since the latter is only considered as a specific form of concreteness of juridicity that, as already seen, is conceived as broader and, moreover, more comprehensive of law. Therefore, following Le Roy (2004 and 2015), it could be stated that the complementary relationship in question is expressed by the fact that juridicity is a kind of "encompassing" of law, seen as a *folk system*, that is, a specific form of concretion of the broader phenomenon.[32]

Therefore, as Eberhard (2001) emphasizes, Étienne Le Roy's "theory of multijuridism" allows for the abandonment of the monological view of the legal phenomenon and the recognition of its "tripodal nature, " that is, the fact that it presents – in any social context – three *fundamentals* that are not reducible or mutually ranked: "General and impersonal norms" (GIN), "models of conduct and behavior" (MCC), and "systems of durable

[32] In this sense, a reflection could be made in parallel to Hyden's proposal (2016). The Swedish author emphasizes that "norms are seen as an overarching concept containing different categories." Therefore, referring to "norms" (social and professional), "rules" (ideological, religious, or private) and "law," the author says that "these different systems of norms interfere with each other in a way that creates a kind of trans-normative reflexivity. Within one and the same formal organization (jurisdiction), national state, there might be competing norms on the same level, e.g. different legal systems or different religious rules."

dispositions" (SDD). Such fundamentals –, which, as we will see, could be articulated in different forms – shape the field of what is legal. In fact, when analyzing what he calls a "legal tripod" (*tripode juridique*), Le Roy (2007) starts from an anthropological approach to Jean Carbonnier's *Flexible Droit*, in which the author proposes two "fundamental theorems" for legal sociology. The first consists in the assertion that the law is greater than its formal sources. The second states that the law is smaller than the set of relations among men.[33] To these two theorems Carbonnier proposed to support his legal sociology, Le Roy (2007; 2009; 2013) adds a third: that juridicity is broader than the concept of law developed in Western societies to encompass it.

Therefore, taking back the two theorems Carbonnier proposed (2001[1969]), Le Roy (2007) introduces the question of juridicity as something that is placed, so to speak, "in the blind spot" of an analysis that, like that of Carbonnier (2001[1969]), expresses a theoretical framework limited to the Western legal tradition. Le Roy (1999, 2007, and 2017) asserts that juridicity manifests a "common domain of regulation" in which the Western experience appears only as a *folk system*, among others. Thus, by pointing out the legitimacy of the multiple forms of concrete expression of juridicity and the impossibility of taking one of them as expressive of the phenomenon as a whole, Le Roy's "theory of multijuridism" provides the possibility of apprehending the complexity of legal regulation beyond its state form of expression.

Le Roy (1998, 1999, 2007; 2009b; 2011c; 2013, and 2017) notes that "general and impersonal norms" (GIN), "models of conduct and behavior" (MCC), and "systems of durable dispositions" (SDD), conceived as three "fundamentals of juridicity," are inherent to all forms of articulation of legality, including that expressed in the Western legal tradition. Therefore, to him the only difference between the different legal traditions is in the form of articulation among these three foundations and their respective mode of legitimation. Furthermore, Le Roy (1999) notes that these three fundamentals are general descriptive categories that correspond,

[33] Carbonnier's two theorems (2001[1969], p. 21-24) are as follows: "Le droit est plus grand que les sources formelles du droit" e "le droit est plus petit que l'ensemble des relations entre les hommes." In this sense, Carbonnier's analysis (2008[1972]) regarding the plurality of normative systems and the phenomena of internormativity is quite illustrative.

respectively, to what is traditionally called law, custom, and *habitus*[34]. The author says that the "general and impersonal norms" (GIN) – that is, those emanating from a center of power –, despite being privileged in the assembly experienced by juridicity within the framework of the modern Western experience, could be considered, metaphorically, only the "emerged part of a legal iceberg," which comprises, on the waterline, the "models of conduct and behavior" (i.e., customs and habits) and, largely immersed in everyday social practices, the "systems of durable dispositions" (the *habitus* as a form of expression of the being, a tuning between behaviors and the frame of the situation).[35]

3. Étienne Le Roy's "theory of multijuridism" as an analytical instrument for "decoding" the "regimes of juridicity" in the context of social exclusion in the Brazilian urban space

This concise presentation of the general aspects of Étienne Le Roy's "theory of multijuridism" allows us to realize the extent to which it is suited to stand as an adequate theoretical framework for the apprehension of the dynamics of regulation (here called "regimes of juridicity") in contexts of social exclusion in the urban space of contemporary Brazil.[36] Regarding this aspect, worthy of note is that, seeking to move away from what he calls theories *prêt-à-penser*, Étienne Le Roy develops an inductive approach based on "participant observation" and field research. However,

[34] Here we can see Pierre Bourdieu's influence on Étienne Le Roy. In Bourdieu (1986), *habitus* is described as a system of durable dispositions directed towards practice (characterized by its spontaneity, vagueness, and imprecision) that is the objective foundation of ordinary conduct. Bourdieu (1986) contrasts the indeterminacy and uncertainty inherent in the *habitus* with the "express rule" that characterizes the codified behaviors. Le Roy (1999 and 2011a) analyzes the concept of *habitus* and specifies his position vis-a-vis Bourdieu's. On this issue, it would be possible to identify in Le Roy's proposal a kind of "jurisdicization" of the *habitus*, through its clear application in the legal field.

[35] Le Roy (1999) also designates these three categories that describe "macronorms," "mesonorms," and "micronorms," respectively. Eberhard (2003, p. 58) criticizes Le Roy's use of these terms, stating that "nous nous demandons, si d'un point de vue pluraliste, il est tout à fait adéquat, comme le fait Étienne Le Roy de ramener les normes générales et impersonnelles à de 'macro-normes', les modèles de conduite et de comportement à de 'méso-normes' et le systèmes de dispositions durables ou habitus à des 'micro-normes'."

[36] It is worth noting that Le Roy (1999) applies his "theory of multijuridism" to the study of *banlieues* in France.

although his field of expertise is land law in Africa, his work is not limited, as Moore (2006) notes, to a narrow empiricism. On the contrary, it is a perspective that, by shaping a sophisticated theoretical elaboration, can significantly contribute to a better understanding of legal regulation in Brazil.

Le Roy (1998 and 1999) emphasizes that even the law, in its modern Western configuration, presents a complex conformation in which "general and impersonal norms" (GIN), "models of conduct and behavior" (MCC), and "systems of durable dispositions" (SDD) coexist.[37] This means that it is not possible to separate – except from an analytical point of view – the three fundamentals: It is, on the contrary, a multiplicity[38]. Therefore, from this perspective, not even Western law – seen as a particular "avatar" of juridicity, that is, as a *folk law* – could be considered coextensive with the field of "general and impersonal norms."[39] According to Le Roy (1998), reducing law to the dimension of the norm would express an idealist conception incompatible with the social complexity that underlies it.[40] Therefore, Étienne Le Roy's "theory of multijuridism," by virtue of its assumptions, has evident affinities with the pluralist conceptions of the legal phenomenon.[41] As Eberhard (2003) emphasizes, these affinities

[37] In this regard, Le Roy (2011c, p. 172) emphasizes "la comparaison des modes de régulation convoqués dans diverses expériences juridiques, en Europe, en Afrique ou en Amérique du Nord m'avait conduit à substituer la notion de fondement à celle de source puis à proposer trois fondements tant du droit que de la juridicité puisque, pour moi, [...] le droit est un avatar particulier de la juridicité, un *folk law* inhérent à la vision moderne de la société."

[38] Le Roy (2003, p. 11-13) asserts that the multiplicity that characterizes the approach to multijuridism "nous situe dans « l'entre-deux » de l'individualisme et du holisme, dans une *multiplicité* qui n'est ni l'unité de l'individu ni la globalité du holisme. D'où la notion de multijuridisme."

[39] As Le Roy (2003, p. 13) emphasizes, "la réalité est complexe et la juridicité est toujours un métissage de régulations."

[40] According to Le Roy (1998, p. 39), "nous considérons en effet que le droit est trípode, qu'il possède trois fondements que les sociétés ne valorisent pas également. Les règles générales, abstraites et impersonnelles sont le matériau de notre conception écrite et 'idéaliste' du Droit."

[41] For approaches that focus on the pluralist debate from its diversity and that contrast the perspectives of Étienne Le Roy and Jacques Vanderlinden, see: Eberhard (2003) and Villas Bôas Filho (2015 and 2015). In this regard, see also: Rouland (1988, 1995, 2003) and Sacco (2007).

become evident if one considers that Le Roy's perspective contributes to the emancipation of the approach to the "legal phenomenon" from its unitary references, such as the State or the legal system, since, as seen, to the "theory of multijuridism" state law is only a particular form of expression of juridicity.

However, compared to theories of legal pluralism, the "theory of multijuridism" also has the advantage of decentering the analysis of the dynamics of regulation in the context of social exclusion from its normative dimension, since it conceives legality as composed not only of "general and impersonal norms" (GIN), but also of "models of conduct and behavior" (MCC) and "systems of durable dispositions" (SDD). In this sense, it is particularly useful to conceive "legal regimes" in contexts characterized by social exclusion, in which it is reasonable to assume that interactions are legally regulated not by "general and impersonal norms" (GIN), but by "models of conduct and behavior" (MCC) and by "systems of durable dispositions" (SDD). In fact, Le Roy's proposal seems to encourage to conceive law and juridicity in a distinctly sociological view, since law and juridicity are seen as a way of acting socially, as a way of social action through meaning (Ferrari, 2010).

Final considerations

Starting from the "theory of multijuridism" proposed by Étienne Le Roy, we focused, in contexts of social exclusion in urban spaces, on "legal regimes", conceived as an expression of different forms of implementation of legal regulation distinct from the State law and which are not predominantly articulated on the basis of "general and impersonal norms." Thus, first, based particularly on the work of Lúcio Kowarick, we briefly addressed the issue of exclusion and socioeconomic and civil vulnerability in the urban space of contemporary Brazil. We then focused on a few fundamental aspects of Étienne Le Roy's "theory of multijuridism." Finally, we tried to emphasize that the "theory of multijuridism" is a very appropriate analytical tool for "decoding" "regimes of juridicity" in characterized by social exclusion.

In this sense, approaches such as Le Roy's show not only that forms of juridicity other than the traditional, Western one, exist; but also that, if taken seriously, they encourage to rethink consolidated semantic categories – such as, for example, those of "citizenship" and "norm" – as they show that these may not be able to adequately describe the multiple social forms and modes of legal regulation that characterize the contemporary world.

Literature

APPADURAI, Arjun. *Il futuro come fatto culturale. Saggi sulla condizione globale.* Milano: Raffaello Cortina, 2014.

ARENDT, Hannah. *The Origins of Totalitarianism.* New York: Harcourt, Brace & World, 1966 [1951].

ARNAUD, André-Jean. Droit et société: un carrefour interdisciplinaire. *Revue Interdisciplinaire d'Études Juridiques,* v. 21, p. 7-32, 1988.

ARNAUD, André-Jean. Droit et société: du constat à la construction d'un champ commun. *Droit et Société,* nº 20-21, p. 17-38, 1992.

BAILLEUX, Antoine; OST, François. Droit, contexte et interdisciplinarité: refondation d'une démarche. *Revue Interdisciplinaire d'Études Juridiques,* v. 70, n. 1, p. 25-44, 2013.

BLANKERTZ, Stefan; GOODMAN, Paul. *Staatlichkeitswahn.* Wetzlar: Büchse der Pandora Verlags, 1980.

BOURDIEU, Pierre. Habitus, code et codification. *Actes de la Recherche en Sciences Sociales,* v. 64, p. 40-44, 1986.

BOURDIEU, Pierre. Esprits d'État [Genèse et structure du champ bureaucratique]. *Actes de la Recherche en Sciences Sociales,* v. 96-97, p. 49-62, Mars. 1993.

BOURDIEU, Pierre. *Raisons pratiques.* Sur la théorie de l'action. Paris: Éditions du Seuil, 1994.

BOURDIEU, Pierre. *Sur l'État.* Cours au Collège de France 1989-1992. Paris: Éditions du Seuil, 2012.

CARBONNIER, Jean. *Flexible droit.* Pour une sociologie du droit sans rigueur. 10. ed. Paris: LGDJ, 2001 [1969].

CARBONNIER, Jean. *Sociologie juridique.* 2. ed. Paris: Presses Universitaires de France, 2008 [1972].

CARVALHO, José Murillo. *Cidadania no Brasil*: o longo caminho. 12ª edição. Rio de Janeiro: Civilização Brasileira, 2009.

CASTEL, Robert. De l'indigence à l'éxclusion, la desaffiliation: précarité du travail et vulnérabilité relationnelle. *In:* DONZELOT, J. (Org.). *Face à l'éxclusion* : le modèle français. Paris: Éditions Esprit, 1991. p. 137-168.

CASTEL, Robert. Les pièges de l'exclusion. *Lien Social et Politiques,* n. 34, p. 13-21, 1995.

CASTEL, Robert. *Les métamorphoses de la question sociale*: une chronique du salariat. Paris: Gallimard, (2003 [1995]).

CORSI, Giancarlo. Redes de la exclusion. *In:* CASTAÑEDA SABIDO, Fernando; CEÉLLAR VÁZQUEZ, Angelica (Orgs.). *Redes de inclusión. La construcción social de la autoridad.* Ciudad de México: Universidad Nacional Autónoma de México,1998, p. 29-42.

CORSI, Giancarlo; DE GIORGI, Raffaele. Perché ridescrivere la Questione Meridionale? In: ______. *Ridescrivere la Questione Meridionale.* Lecce: Pensa Multimedia Editore, 1998, p. 7-90.

DE GIORGI, Raffaele. Redes da inclusão. *In: Direito, democracia e risco. Vínculos com o futuro.* Porto Alegre: Sergio Antonio Fabris Editor, 1998, p. 133-148.

DE GIORGI, Raffaele. Evoluzione della fiducia e periferie dell'accadere: *Quaderno di comunicazione.* Dipartimento di Filosofia e Scienze sociali dell'Università di Lecce, n. 6, p. 11-23, 2006.

DE GIORGI, Raffaele. Periferias da modernidade. *Revista Direito Mackenzie,* v. 11, n. 2, p. 39-47, 2017.

DUMONT, Hugues; BAILLEUX, Antoine. Esquisse d'une théorie des ouvertures interdisciplinaires accessibles aux juristes. *Droit et Société,* n. 75, p. 275-293, 2010.

EBERHARD, Christoph. Towards an intercultural legal theory: the dialogical challenge. *Social & Legal Studies,* v. 2, n. 2, p. 171-201, 2001.

EBERHARD, Christoph. Penser le pluralisme juridique de manière pluraliste. Défi pour une théorie interculturelle du droit. *Cahiers d'Anthropologie du Droit 2003* (Les pluralismes juridiques). Paris: Karthala, 2003, p. 51-63.

EBERHARD, Christoph. *Le droit au miroir des cultures.* Pour une autre mondialisation. Paris: LGDJ, 2010.

FARIA, José Eduardo. Estado, sociedade e direito. *In:* FARIA, José Eduardo; KUNTZ, Rolf. *Qual o futuro dos direitos?* Estado, mercado e justiça na reestruturação capitalista. São Paulo: Max Limonad, 2002. p. 59-130.

FARIA, José Eduardo. *Sociologia jurídica*: direito e conjuntura. São Paulo: Saraiva, 2010.

FASSIN, Didier. Exclusion, underclass, marginalidad: figures contemporaines de la pauvreté urbaine en France, aux États-Unis et en Amérique Latine. *Review Française de Sociologie,* v. 37, p. 37-75, 1996.

FEBBRAJO, Alberto (Org.). *Sociologia del diritto. Concetti e problemi.* Bologna: il Mulino, 2013.

FEBBRAJO, Alberto (Org.). Tre definizioni del concetto di diritto. *In:* EHRLICH, Eugene; KELSEN, Hans; WEBER, Max. *Verso in concetto sociologico di diritto.* Milano: Giuffrè, 2010.

FERRARI, Vincenzo. *Prima lezione di sociologia del diritto.* Roma-Bari: Laterza, 2010.

HARVEY, David. The Right to the City. *New Left Review,* 53, p. 23-40, 2008.

HYDÉN, Håkan. *The Normative Anatomy of Society,* manuscrito, setembro, 2016.

KOWARICK, Lúcio. Viver em risco – sobre a vulnerabilidade no Brasil urbano. *Novos Estudos* – Cebrap, n. 63, p. 9-30, jul. 2002.

KOWARICK, Lúcio. *Viver em risco*: sobre a vulnerabilidade socioeconômica e civil. São Paulo: Editora 34, 2009.

LE ROY, Étienne. L'hypothèse du multijuridisme dans un contexte de sortie de la modernité. *In:* LAJOIE, Andrée; MACDONALD, Roderick A.; JANDA, Richard; ROCHER, Guy. *Théories et émergence du droit*: pluralisme, surdétermination et effectivité. Bruxelles: Thémis/Bruylant, 1998. p. 29-43.

LE ROY, Étienne. *Le jeu des lois*. Une anthropologie "dynamique" du Droit. Paris: LGDJ, 1999.

LE ROY, Étienne. Le pluralisme juridique aujourd'hui ou l'enjeu de la juridicité. *Cahiers d'Anthropologie du Droit 2003* (Les pluralismes juridiques). Paris: Karthala, 2003. p. 7-15.

LE ROY, Étienne. Pour une anthropologie de la juridicité. *Cahiers d'Anthropologie du Droit 2004* (Anthropologie et droit – intersections et confrontations). Paris: Karthala, 2004. p. 241-247.

LE ROY, Étienne. Le tripode juridique. Variations anthropologiques sur un thème de flexible droit. *L'Année Sociologique*, n. 2, v. 57, p. 341-351, 2007.

LE ROY, Étienne. Autonomie du droit, hétéronomie de la juridicité. *In:* SACCO, Rodolfo (ed.). *Le nuove ambizioni del sapere del giurista*: antropologia giuridica e traduttologia giuridica. Roma: Accademia Nazionale dei Lincei, 2009. p. 99-133.

LE ROY, Étienne. *La terre de l'autre*. Une anthropologie des régimes d'appropriation foncière. Paris: LGDJ, 2011a.

LE ROY, Étienne. La révolution de la juridicité, une réponse aux mondialisations. *Paper* referente à comunicação realizada no II Encontro Nacional de Antropologia do Direito, realizado na Universidade de São Paulo em 31 de agosto de 2011. 2011b, p. 1-21. Mimeographed.

LE ROY, Étienne. Les fondements de la socialisation juridique, entre droit et juridicité. *Cahiers d'Anthropologie du Droit 2010* (Pratiques citoyennes de droit). Paris: Karthala, 2011c. p. 169-192.

LE ROY, Étienne. Place de la juridicité dans la médiation. *Jurisprudence – Revue Critique*, n. 4 *(La médiation. Entre renouvellement de l'offre de justice et droit)*, p. 193-208, 2013.

LE ROY, Étienne. Les appropriations de terres à grande échelle et les politiques foncières au regard de la mondialisation d'un droit en crise. *Droit et Société*, n. 82, p. 193-206, 2015.

LE ROY, Étienne. *Une juridicité plurielle pour le XXe siècle*. Une approche anthropologique d'une propédeutique juridique. Sarrebruck: Éditions Universitaires Européennes, 2017.

LUHMANN, Niklas. Globalization or World society: How to conceive of modern society?. *International Review of Sociology*, v. 7, issue 1, p. 67-79, mar 1997.

LUHMANN, Niklas. Causalità nel Sud. *In:* DE GIORGI, Raffaele; CORSI, Giancarlo. *Ridescrivere la questione meridionale*. Lecce: Pensa Multimedia Editore, p. 91-125, 1998.

LUHMANN, Niklas. Inclusão e exclusão. *In:* DUTRA, Roberto; BACHUR, João Paulo (Orgs.). *Dossiê Niklas Luhmann*. Belo Horizonte: Editora da UFMG, 2013, p. 15-50.

MOORE, Sally Falk. The Sociologic of Land Law. *In:* EBERHARD, Christoph; VERNICOS, Geneviève (Ed.). *La quête anthropologique du droit*. Autour de la démarche d'Étienne Le Roy. Paris: Karthala, 2006, p. 133-145.

RICOTTA, Giuseppe. Ripensare l'emancipazione sociale: sociologia della assenze e delle emergenze. *Quaderni di Teoria Sociale*, n. 1, p. 179-198, 2019.

ROSANVALLON, Pierre. *La nouvelle question sociale*: repenser l'État-providence. Paris: Éditions du Seuil, 1995.

ROSANVALLON, Pierre. *La légitimité démocratique*: impartialité, réflexivité, proximité. Paris: Éditions du Seuil, 2008.

ROULAND, Norbert. *Anthropologie juridique*. Paris: Presses Universitaires de France, 1988.

ROULAND, Norbert. *L'anthropologie juridique*. Paris: Presses Universitaires de France, 1995.

ROULAND, Norbert. *Nos confins do direito*. Tradução de Maria Ermantina de Almeida Prado Galvão. São Paulo: Martins Fontes, 2003.

SACCO, Rodolfo. *Antropologia giuridica*: contributo ad una macrostoria del diritto. Bologna: Il Mulino, 2007

SANTOS, Boaventura de Sousa. *Para um novo senso comum*: a ciência, o direito e a política na transição paradigmática. A crítica da razão indolente: contra o desperdício da experiência. 4. ed. São Paulo: Cortez, 2002a. v. 1.

SANTOS, Boaventura de Sousa. Para uma sociologia das ausências e uma sociologia das emergências. *Revista Crítica de Ciências Sociais*, 63, p. 237-280, 2002b.

SANTOS, Boaventura de Sousa. *Epistemologies of the South: Justice Against Epistemicide*. New York: Routledge, 2014.

SANTOS, Boaventura de Sousa. *The End of the Cognitive Empire. The Coming of Age of Epistemologies of the South*. Duke University Press, 2018.

SOUZA, Jessé. *A construção social da subcidadania*: para uma sociologia política da modernidade periférica. Belo Horizonte: Editora UFMG; Rio de Janeiro: IUPERJ, 2003.

TOURAINE, Alain. *In difesa della modernità*. Milano: Raffaello Cortina, 2019.

VILLAS BÔAS FILHO, Orlando. Juridicidade: uma abordagem crítica à monolatria jurídica enquanto obstáculo epistemológico. *Revista da Faculdade de Direito da USP*, v. 109, p. 281-325, jan./dez. 2014.

VILLAS BÔAS FILHO, Orlando. A regulação jurídica para além de sua forma ocidental de expressão: uma abordagem a partir de Étienne Le Roy. *Direito & Práxis*, v. 6, n. 12, p. 159-195, 2015.

VILLAS BÔAS FILHO, Orlando. A mediação em um campo de análise interdisciplinar: o aporte da teoria do multijuridismo de Étienne Le Roy. *Revista Estudos Institucionais*, v. 3, n. 2, p. 1112-1162, 2017.

VILLAS BÔAS FILHO, Orlando. A análise antropológica no âmbito dos estudos sociojurídicos: aportes para a construção de um campo interdisciplinar. *Pensamento Jurídico*, v. 12, n. 2, p. 9-38, 2018a.

VILLAS BÔAS FILHO, Orlando. O desenvolvimento dos estudos sociojurídicos: da cacofonia à construção de um campo de pesquisa interdisciplinar. *Revista da Faculdade de Direito da Universidade de São Paulo*, v. 113, p. 251-292, jan./dez. 2018b.

VILLAS BÔAS FILHO, Orlando. Desafios da pesquisa interdisciplinar: as ciências sociais como instrumentos de "vigilância epistemológica" no campo dos estudos sociojurídicos. *Revista Estudos Institucionais*, v. 5, n. 2, p. 530-558, 2019.

VILLAS BÔAS FILHO, Orlando. O Estado como instituição responsável pela (re)produção e canonização das formas de classificação social: notas sobre a tese de Pierre Bourdieu. *In:* FEBBRAJO, Alberto *et al.* (coord.). *Sociologia jurídica*: novas observações sobre problemas fundamentais. Curitiba: Juruá, 2021. p. 119-136.

4. CREATIVE AND SOCIAL INNOVATIVE POTENTIALITIES IN SÃO PAULO: GRAFFITI CASE AND THE REGULATED TRANSFORMATION OF URBAN SPACE

Irene Nohara
Carlos Leite
Elisabete Castanheira

Introduction: Analysis Context

The present paper focus on the urban artistic manifestation's agenda at São Paulo city through graffiti from two complementary approaches.

The first part of the paper deals with the conceptual issue of the theme, which is associated with the creative and socially innovative potentialities of such manifestations in a contemporary city. For several years, urban territory at Brazilian largest city and in line with international trend at large urban centers stands as support for various non-formal creative manifestation (in strict sense of the term). Several arrangements of artistic collective use to rethink the supports of their productions and manifestations from urban scale perspective.

Art and city and art in the contemporary city are manifestations that lead us to the following questions: after all, who owns the urban space? Or, what are the legal limits and possibilities of such manifestations? What is the possible regulation of graffiti considered as a contemporary artistic manifestation that is typical of the city? The first questions are going to be faced at the first part of the paper and the last of the questions is going to be object of the second one.

In which context does these artistic manifestations arise, as they have the city as their support? These are phenomena which have been studied by many researchers for several years, under a muti and interdisciplinary approach, and that can still be contemplated under the specific approach of *creative city*.

Metropolises are a *locus* of diversity: from economy to ideology, through religion, culture and art. Big cities generate creative spatial externalities that have, for instance, stimulated urban economy researches like Jane Jacobs, the Canadian who pioneered the potential of urban diversity that cities like her beloved New York brought as a differential for economic growth and wealth of collective live, also Edward Glaeser, Harvard Urban Economist, that emphasized economic externalities that contemporary metropolises provide; from Richard Florida, urban economist who developed the concept of *creative cities,* and to the Nobel Prize in economics, Paul Krugman, who associates the major urban densities as causes of urban externalities.

This is not just a concept used for developed cities as the spatial externalities approach may have been based on international research focusing on successful experiences of large cities from the northern hemisphere, as New York, Montreal, Barcelona and San Francisco, but it is applied as well as to south cities. There are promising indicators also presented in large cities like São Paulo or Mumbai. Furthermore, is observed that signs of positive spatial externalities flourish in the so-called informal territories, from Heliópolis, in São Paulo, to Dharavi in Mumbas (LEITE, 2012).

It is also worth emphasize the important character, both in urban creative manifestation and in their forms of formal regulation – of social interaction as reflexive cooperation emerging in such context, according to LEVY and LEITE (2020):

> Cooperation between citizens who appreciate each other and also recognize themselves as socially useful. And, finally, it leads to a cooperative democratic structure, equally performed with transformative potential, beyond formal and institutional structures of democratic representation and participation. This is an important difference to the regulation dimension, insofar as the law's legitimacy is strengthened when the main ones affected can participate in its formulation and assent to its content.

The present paper approaches the multi and interdisciplinary agenda of the city, project and equity, considering the languages and appropriations of its forms of regulation, through the creative and socially innovative potentialities in São Paulo. The main objective is to focus on the case study of graffiti regulation, through its legal limits and possibilities and the approach of socialpolitical governance of the transformation from urban space by art and culture, which is mediated by legal regulation of the subject.

1. Creative and socially innovative potentialities in São Paulo

Through different dynamics, including subsystems, the city is configurated as a contemporary complexity. It is in this context that emerges new forms of interactions. These forms are self-organized and they acquire remarkable behavior given the ability to transform its configuration and, above all, the uses that citizens have made of the city.

One of these forms of interaction happens through artistic intervention, which means appropriate to make art.

More than providing deep change in art, the context of the 20th century, as a multiple artistic manifestation, allowed the expansion of spaces destined for its realization and enjoyment, in the so called, by Sevcenko (2001), panorama of the *dematerialization of artistic supports*.

Artists and artistic collectives from São Paulo are usually rethinking the supports of their productions from a scale perspective: focusing on the urban scale.

BijaRi, from São Paulo, is one of these agents that transform urban space through artistic intervention. The ecletic collective seeks to discuss the idea of belonging. After all, the main question to be asked is: who in fact owns the urban space?

This reflection actually take place in several ways, such as, the transformation of abandoned cars at São Paulo streets into real gardens; the collage of creative messages (which is called, in street slang of São Paulo "lambe"); or the Praças (Im)Possíveis Project, based on the installation of using equipment like bicycles with beach chairs placed on unlikely places like under the viaduct; and also works that stimulate the discussion about gentrification, which includes occupation of unused properties and other urban dynamics.

City, art and urban appropriation, in São Paulo, are concepts that are immediately associated with graffiti and street art. It is quite rare to dissociate them. On the other hand, approaching art and the city are ideas that remind the borders of what is public compared to private.

Further than a space for citizen's transit, public is a concept that marks all places as the materialization of coexistence (living together), interaction, encounter, fruition and especially expression. Still, private property is often vulnerable to the desire of the appropriator and can be transformed into an artistic support, raising debates in different spheres, as it is difficult to gather consensus. It is a dimension that not always allow forms of dialogue and even understanding on the matter.

However, urban intervention, whatever it may be, is always a result that communicates and changes, not only the space, but all of those who are involved in the process.

An essentially typographic manifestation, which is called in portuguese *pichação* (*pixação* or even *pixo*), is an intervention process, emanated from the edge of the city and whose motivations includes the search for identity, belonging, among many others, and, precisely for this reason, it must be accompanied by 'brand', that is to say, the signature which identifies the group to which the tagger belongs, and, in whose essence, are the principles to be followed (PEREIRA, 2010).

Despite coexisting in São Paulo, pixo and graffiti are antagonized by the growing understanding that graffiti, unlike pixo, can materialize an artwork. Abroad, this dichotomy does not exist, constituting only classifications for the same artistic language.

While for some people, pixo is considered a transgression, for the activity of the tagger is based on social contestation and the only possible certainty of belonging. It is a way to guide and explain exclusion through plastic, social and urban expressions.

Although it may refer to the idea of a recent urban intervention, graffity already inhabited the walls of ancient Rome and renewed its prominence in the 1970s, in the United Sates, in the hands of Keith Haring and Basquiat.

In Brazil, at the same period, it was up to Alex Vallauri to appropriate the city as a support for his graphic expression, an initiative which was later followed by Ruy Amaral, Speto, Os Gêmeos, Kobra, Crânio, among many other artists, often anonymous.

Give me Light, Picasso de Delftsehof, Spetö/2009 Brbbl.

From: Festival de Rotterdam

This is an expression that carries a strong São Paulo imprinting, establishing the gray urban in a transversal way. Center and edge, edge and center, are presented under these large-scale signs, not always easy to understand. For some, such brands are integrated into the buildings, as they always belonged there. For others, on the other hand, they are considered quite invasive. All forms of appropriation result from a new understanding of the city, which goes far beyond what is visible, and shows itself through what is not yet there, but will be, if it is desired and undertaken (CASTANHEIRA, 2019).

2. Regulation of graffiti: legal limits and possibilities

Pichação, pixo or *pixação*, in portuguese, is considered a crime. According to Public Law nº 9.605 (article 56), with the text altered by Public Law nº 12.408/2011, in crimes against urban planning and cultural heritage, *pichação* is seen as "defiling" and as a result it is punished with detention from three months up to one year, plus fine. The penalty is increased if the pixo is held at a monument or thing that has been listed for its artistic, archaeological or historical value. Its different from the legal regulation of graffiti, which has been decriminalized in Brazil.

Pichação is the forbidden act of painting or scratching walls, objects and buildings whereas graffiti, as an art manifestation, is not considered a crime, as long as it is carried out with the objective of valuing public or private heritage through artistic expression, with the consent of the owner or, when applicable, of the tenant from the private property.

It should be warned that, in the case of public goods, there must be a formal authorization from the competent body and also in compliance with municipal posture, as well with rules issued by government bodies responsible for the preservation and conservation of the national historical and artistic heritage, as established in art. 56, § 6º, of Public Act nº 9.605/1996, with the addition of Public Act nº 12.408/2011.

The movement to decriminalize graffiti was driven by the progressive recognition of its artistic characteristic, which generated growing appreciation of the public, despite some more conservative sectors of society still see it as a visual pollution. Thus, the practice is commonly associated with vandalism.

On the other hand, a more progressive bias envisions the beautiful effect of graffiti, as it can be used as a potential to ornament both private and public goods, especially in São Paulo, which is a city that brings together renowned artists of national and international recognition.

Therefore, at the same time of decriminalization of graffiti and the progressive recognition of its artistic and cultural value in the city, due to its value as an urban art manifestation, especially applied to murals, it was noticed that it causes, in the end, the appreciation of spaces, and has a great value being associated with specific actions of aesthetic transformation of urban space.

Graffiti is an artistic expression which is generally associated with the "counterculture" as well as with hip hop. It has acquired recognition as an alternative form of expression in New York and Europe from the 1970s onwards. Afterwards, graffiti achieved aesthetic taste and, therefore, collective appreciation in large South American metropolises, such as São Paulo (BOEMER, 2013; LARA, 1996, p. 50).

North American graffiti is associated with an artistic expression that reflects urban live (street art), with a proper focus on themes of social exclusion. Despite the inspiration, Brazilian graffiti has acquired its own manifestations, being currently recognized as one of the best in the world.

Paulista Tunnel, which is the underpass that connects Paulista Avenue to Doutor Arnaldo, is the pionner place opened to graffiti since the eighties. It has been historically transformed and maintained as a huge graphite panel.

The first artist who left his imprint at the place was Rui Amaral,[1] who painted big robots and spaceships. At that time, he was arrested while working and spent nights in jail. However, when completed, his art was accepted by public (and authorities) and it was also so valued that it had already undergone through six restorations to acquire permanence in the location.

It is important to point out that the institutionalization of graffiti took place in the time which Luiza Erundina (1989-1992) was São Paulo's Mayor, as she was the first chief to formally encourage the practice.

Grafite from Rui Amaral.

Photo by André Deak. From: Arte fora do Museu.

[1] Guide of expositions. Available on: https://guia-de-exposicoes-blog.tumblr.com/post/22272853239/o-buraco-da-paulista-interven%C3%A7%C3%A3o-olhar.

Due to the 453rd anniversary of São Paulo, Paulista Tunnel received an intervention of 140 urban artists who, for 2008, painted a mural measuring 430 linear meters or 2.200 square meters in celebration of the Japanese Centenary Immigration. The project was entitled the "Rising Eye" and it concentrated an axis that represented the Japanese history, aesthetics and legends through three meters high images.

Another well-known place in São Paulo that gathers tourism and cultural life, and which has used graffiti as a stimulus, is the so-called "Batman's Alley", which is located at Vila Madalena's bohemian neighborhood. It is a place that brings together paintings from different styles of artists.

As it was emphasized, graffiti causes opposing postures on people. While some people admire it and appreciate it, there are those who do not appreciate or even despise it, having, thus, strong resistance accepting its extension use at urban spaces.

In order to achieve a greater degree of legitimacy within the legal frameworks that regulate its practice, graffiti should be associated with the consent of owners, lessees and tenants and even if it is a public space it will demand authorization from the competent body, provided that the municipal regulations and also the rules issued by legal bodies responsible for conservation are strictly observed.

According to Marcílio Toscano Franca Filho, graffiti is traditionally associated with the following notes: marginality, anonymity, spontaneity, cenerity, speed, precariousness and fleetingness. However, not all of the mentioned characteristics are always presented at urban center graffiti, because there are popular artists that end up wanting to leave the anonymity and, as a result, having their name associated with the art they produce.

As the number of connoisseurs increases, people also start to order graffiti. Marcílio explains that: "often, governments, individuals and private companies use to order panels from famous or even anonymous graffiti artists, who carefully elaborate their pieces, so that they remain long" (FRANCA FILHO, 2016).

Unfortunately, spontaneity can also be affected by the excess of requirements demanded by the regulation of graffiti, which raises the following consideration: could the excess of bureaucratization from graffiti harm its free spirit, counterculture and appreciation of "art for art´s sake"?

From this perspective, there are inconsistencies in the attempt of qualifying or disqualifying art. However, it cannot be denied that, at the same time that graphite suffers a more intensive regulatory burden, the competent bodies must also take care not to exceed the quantity of requirements, so that they do not harm the essential core of artistic freedom,[2] belittling it by restricting it to the function of commissioned art, both in form and, even worse, in the content (HÄBERLE, 2003, p. 58).

The problem with the excess of rules and the limit on its manifestation causes an accommodation that represents a downgrading on the freedom that characterizes graffiti. Regarding this problem, there are no ready answers, but one can point out some guidelines and suggestions from governance point of view in order to preserve the freedom of expression, as long as this freedom don't collide with the consensus that should emerge from urban interventions, given the potential clash between freedoms.

So, affected groups can be dived into: (1) artists, who, due to creative stimulation, must have preserved the possibility of manifestation with an adequate degree of freedom; (2) owners or lessees of the public or private property that will have the graffiti art, who should have respected their consent to the practice; and (3) citizens who will have access to and enjoy (or not) such form of artistic and cultural expression.

It is therefore required a reasonable regulation of graffiti, which harmonizes the various interests. The regulation should provoke means of recognition of the potential for transformation of urban space through graffiti, especially when it is associated with certain public policies, as it will be exposed below.

3. Final Considerations: sociopolitical governance of urban space transformation and social inclusion through graffiti

Graffiti is an artistic and cultural expression that has the potential to contribute to the transformation and ornamentation of the city. However, as a duty to its regular practice, there is a need to respect the framework of the legality in the broadest sense. It still can be associated with several projects, which allows the activity to be carried out with greater security without provoking liability or even abuses by public authorities.

[2] Therefore, in order to reach agreement in certain cases, especially dealing with private orders, there is a need to verify its execution in advance, but in others physical spaces can be provided for artists to work with greater freedom in the creation of graffiti.

Thus, it is important to raise public manager awareness about the potential of adding graffiti to the governance arrangement in order to bring visibility to public projects, which is an opportunity to stimulate the creativity as well as to engage street art in public policies with the scope of increasing the enjoyment of the city.

There are social projects that can associate graffiti to stimulate the creativity of street art, as well as to increase the visibility and fruition from the cultural experience of the city. An example to be highlighted in São Paulo is the *ballet dancers' stairs* painted by the renowned artist Eduardo Kobra.

This is an intervention that took place on the staircase nicknamed "escadão", which is located at Alves Guimarães Street, in Pinheiros District, between Teodoro Sampaio and Cardeal Arcoverde Streets, in which the artist painted ballet dancers inspired by the painter Degás.

However, they are not random dancers, as some of them are actually members of the Ballet Paraisópolis, with Paraisópolis being a low income community located near Morumbi neighborhood. The social and cultural project Ballet Paraisópolis manages to select talented ballet dancers for training and also for performances.

Ballet Dancer Mel Reis.

From: R7 Photographer Edu Garcia

Due to the project ballerinas conducted by Kobra's graffiti art there was a connection between Pinheiros Neighborhood and the cultural happenings at Paraisópolis. So, graffiti can also be viewed as a relevant offensive to publicize the social inclusion projects, given the visibility which is linked with.

Kobra's art was so appreciated that the staircase was included into the tourist visitation circuit of São Paulo, raising visibility for the Paraisópolis ballet itself. During the opening, in November 2018, the members of Ballet Paraisópolis performed their choreography on the spot.

From the point of view of private sector, the same artist (Kobra) was once hired to paint the entrance of Leonardo da Vinci's exhibition at the MIS Experience, in São Paulo. It was an art remarkably creative, given the painting showed the creator (Leonardo da Vinci) graffitied on the panel by his creature: Monalisa, which resulted in the expansion of the exhibition's publicity.

However, when business or commercial use of graffiti is raised as an element of urban transformation, there are limits to be respected due to São Paulo's Clean City Law. When adding advertising campaigns or references from commercial brands to the arts, it is forbidden to appear in public spaces at the same form of the disinterested arts, as there are restrictions in relation to the placement of billboards or branding in the city of São Paulo, so it's not allowed to a brand to take a ride on the legitimacy visibility achieved by graffiti (PIRES & SANTOS, 2018).

Graffiti must be developed in an orderly manner, whether it is made in private space or in public space. In São Paulo, Municipal Council for the Preservation of Historical, Cultural and Environmental Heritage of São Paulo (Conpresp) is the body responsible for determining the limits and also for controlling the creation of graffiti. As a result, the Municipality of São Paulo cannot erase the city's graffiti without the consent of Conpresp.

São Paulo is a financial center in Latin America, being highlighted for concentrating a large volume of services. It is estimated to have 12 million inhabitants (IBGE, 2018).[3] It is also a city that brings together similar characteristics of large metropolis, such as New York, and also Asian

[3] Is the most populous Municipality in the country. Available at: https://agenciadenoticias.ibge.gov.br/agencia-sala-de-imprensa/2013-agencia-de-noticias/releases/22374-ibge-divulga-as--estimativas-de-populacao-dos-municipios-para-2018. Access in 20 march 2020.

capitals, being, therefore, a global, cosmopolitan city that gathers both opportunities as well as social exclusion and inequality.

Therefore, in addition to bringing together a large number of graffiti artists, the city is a scene of potential conflict, given the existing gaps in policies to stimulate awareness of the cultural value of graffiti. To illustrate this idea, which reveals a blind spot, a few years ago the Court of Justice of the State of São Paulo condemned[4] the Municipality of São Paulo for removing the graffiti from 23 de Maio Avenue, ordering that the value of the conviction be reversed to São Paulo Cultural and Environmental Heritage Protection Fund.

It is a precedent that represents the judicial recognition of cultural manifestation from graffiti and, as result, that removal without the consent of the competent body represents a damage to cultural heritage. Furthermore, from a positive and promotional point of view, graffiti can be, as it was said, associated with projects that end up enhancing goals through the visibility attached.

In this sense, the project implemented in East Zone of São Paulo, called *graffiti against garbage*, is a successful case. It was an example that generated a bottom-up public management, which represented the incentive of democratic elements.

In Emelino Matarazzo, at Císper Street, located on the East Zone of the city, there was a wall that was once transformed into a place of garbage and rubble disposal. The space was revitalized based on the project led by local Subprefecture, together with Soma consortium, responsible for urban cleaning in the region, with the active participation of urban groups, which was made through proper garbage disposal and especially though calling graffiti artists to color the wall.[5]

The project engaged 320 graffiti artists, which were called to color 700 meters of wall. The event was sealed with the inauguration of the revitalized space. Thus, all of the collectives involved carried out awareness actions for proper disposal of garbage, as the inauguration included an

[4] Available at: https://g1.globo.com/sp/sao-paulo/noticia/2019/02/26/justica-de-sp-condena-doria-e-a-prefeitura-por-remocao-de-grafites-na-23-de-maio.ghtml. Access in 20 march 2020.

[5] Graffiti x Garbage. Available at: https://www.youtube.com/watch?v=zabSHzRc7LY. Access in 20 march 2020.

educational and social orientation offensive, which happened after the cleansing of the place.

The cleansing was done by the work of Soma consortium. The graffiti artists, in turn, colored the entire extension of the wall. As a result, the artistic and cultural agenda was associated with urban environmental sustainability.

Such was the enthusiasm from part of the residents with the realization of the project in their street that many of them also requested the artists to draw graffiti on the gates of their homes located in front of the wall. It can be seen, then, in this project, that there was as stimulus to reach a socialpolitical dimension of the governance.

Instead of the Municipality determining from top to bottom a simple cleansing made by the consortium, there was a special concern with the engagement of multiple social actors (collectives) and from this consultation the project actually achieved not only environmental objectives of urban cleansing, but also sociocultural and artistic goals through spontaneous and provoked creative elements.

Thus, both Municipality can separate public spaces to induce freer expression of urban art in outdoor murals, and graffiti can also be ordered. It is important that the police receive the training and awareness that graffiti art is not forbidden in Brazil.

Furthermore, an option of great effectiveness is that of projects such as *color+city*,[6] which encourage graffiti lovers to give up a private space for art, making it possible, therefore, to choose a wall, a façade or a free space to be painted. Based on this project, it is possible to offer the location, with photos linked to digital media, so that the artist can choose the place where the graffiti will be performed.

It is a democratic project, as the individual offers the space and the artist is free to choose to develop his art freely. The owner of the space can eventually talk to the artist and arrange something, as long as the autonomy of the art creation is respected. Then, added to the realization of art, there may also be the development of apps bounded with tourist itineraries, which can be made by bicycle or even by foot, in which the

[6] Available at: https://sao-paulo.estadao.com.br/noticias/geral,site-encontra-muro-para-grafiteiro-imp-,1115042. Access in 15th March 2020.

artist' data and the characteristics of the mural art is disposed accompany by specific data to inform the public.

Public Administration can lead the project, being an actor responsible for uniting collectives around the implementation of policies in public space, while the private sector can offer spaces to stimulate the artists creativity, as long as it does not abuse graffiti as a way of propagating brands beyond the limits of Clean City Law. Another way of stimulating art, is to encourage the third sector to incorporate graffiti in its manifestations, as in the mentioned case of *the dancers' stairs*, which generated visibility to social projects and at the same time exposed the graffiti art.

New apps are technologies that allow the dissemination of information about itineraries and cultural circuits. Another point to be highlighted is that public authorities should be stimulated to respect the artist's work and to preserve street art, as a lesson extracted from the judicial precedent that condemned São Paulo Municipality that erased the rich graffiti located on 23 de Maio Avenue.

To sum up, graffiti cannot be carried out against the will of individuals, nether can it de-characterize public spaces. If there is a stimulus for its expression, in compliance to the adequate regulation, it's able to reach a potential of transforming spaces and the experiences associated with urban spaces. Graffiti can modify the reactions and the vision one has of the city, which can change the gray scenario of metropolis such as São Paulo, that should have in graffiti a mean of beautifying and humanizing urban landscape, adding identity and also stimulating visibility to associated projects.

References

Boemer, O. F. (2013). *Graffiti como Meio: Processo de Criação entre Sistemas – a lei, a rua, e mercado e a pesquisa em arte*. São Paulo: Unesp.

Castanheira, Elisabete. (2019). *Cidade, porosidade, proposição e prática – cartografia de potencialidades criativas e socialmente inovadoras no centro expandido de São Paulo*. São Paulo: Mackenzie.

Matthews, J. (1999). *The art of childhood and adolescence – the construction of meaning*. London, England: Falmer Press.

Franca Filho, Marcílio Toscano (2016). O grafite e a preservação de sua integridade – a pele da cidade e o *droit au respect* no direito brasileiro e comparado. *Revista de Direito da Cidade*, 8 (4), 1344-1361.

Häberle, P. (2003). *La garantia del contenido essencial de los derechos fundamentales.* Madrid: Dykinson.

Lara, A. H. (1996). *Grafite arte em movimento.* São Paulo: Eca/USP.

Leite, Carlos (2012). *Cidades Sustentáveis, Cidades Inteligentes.* Porto Alegre: Bookman.

Levy, Wilson; Leite, Carlos. Interação, democracia e governança urbanas. Retrieved Set 15, from http://vitruvius.com.b/revistas/read/arquitextos/20.237/7640.

Peixoto, N. B. (1996). *Paisagens Urbanas.* São Paulo: Senac.

Pereira, A. B. (2010). As marcas da cidade: a dinâmica da pichação em São Paulo. *Lua Nova, Revista de Cultura e Política,* from http://scielo.br/pdf/ln/n79/a07n79.pdf/.

Pires, E. M.; Santos, F. A. dos. (2018). A cidade de São Paulo e suas dinâmicas: graffiti, Lei Cidade Limpa e publicidade urbana. *Anais do Museu Paulista,* 26 (11), 1-37. doi: 10.1590/1982-02672018v26e28

Ronconi, Luciana. (2011). Governança Pública: um desafio à democracia. *Emancipação,* 11 (1), 21-34.

Sevcenko, Nicolau. (2001). *A corrida para o século XXI: no loop da montanha russa.* São Paulo: Companhia das Letras.

5. UNIVERSITY PROJECTS AND HUMAN MOBILITY, CONTEMPORARY PERSPECTIVES FOR A CITY THAT CAN EDUCATE AND ACCOMMODATE

Ingrid Hötte Ambrogi
Rosana M. P.B. Schwuartz
João Clemente de S. Neto
Axel Föller
Bianka Mieskes
Bernhard Johannes Fichtner

To think about the role of the university in the contemporary world is to be connected with broader issues that permeate territories and dialogue with global perspectives, such as migration and immigration flows, scarcity, poverty, violence that occur across the planet.

The possibilities created by the PRINT Mackenzie – Alanus Program established the exchange of views and proposals by universities in facing an increasingly intense reality.

In this way, it is a fundamental role of the university to build an interface that allows for integration and alleviates the issues of isolation and segregation with migrants, immigrants, different social realities, by understanding in a more comprehensive manner the dilemmas that permeate issues like these.

Based on this assumption, we point out some important projects carried out in the two countries involved, Brazil and Germany, that even though have great cultural differences, become closer in seeking integration paths and reception processes in the territories, wich in this case, specially reveal the dilemmas of the cities.

Initially, it is necessary to discuss the subject's bond with their territory, what this represents in terms of personal construction, identity and the reasons that lead to the rupture of these roots, whether this fact represents a loss, a great personal challenge or not.

There is always the challenge of understanding the migration/immigration process, poverty, segregation, social and cultural barriers as opposed to the search for integration, this requires a great effort from everyone.

Thus, there is the need to understand a city's place in a person's life, their roots and places of memory, the meanings attributed to places full of personal meanings, built throughout life in different institutions.

Cities are considered the greatest artifact built by human beings, in this sense, regardless of culture as subjects, we build our gatherings in multiple ways, but the results possess similar motivations, whether by the union between people for exchange and mutual protection, or by the need for coexistence inherent to the human being.

Brazilian geographer Milton Santos understands humans relationship with space as an appropriation in the face of forces that emerge in the dispute for its domain, and in a more comprehensive way, over the territory, be it through hegemony in conducting interpersonal relationships or through the conquest of power.

Therefore, to understand how this aspect happens, it is necessary to reveal these interconnections and the multiple feelings that emerge from a given context, how the forces and disputes are constituted in relation to the groups that cohabit a territory.

The understanding of the concept of traditional territory alludes to ownership, whether it's by animals or by man. However, this concept is expanded with authors such as Milton Santos, by attributing social aspects to the territory, the search to understand the contradictory and symbolic forces of power, generating greater dynamism to the concept. These concepts gain greater fluidity especially by attributing meanings beyond the more static physical ones and observing superpositions of forces related to the search for hegemony of multiple territories.

Another author to be evoked is Kevin Lynch, with his book The image of the city (1960), the result of a study of three American cities, in which he attributes the recognition of cities by people through the formation of mental maps, which are formed from the personal experiences and stories.

Lynch recognized the use of beacons he raised with different profiles of people he interviewed in his studies.

For the author, the recognition of the city is done by: 1- **ways** and paths for displacement, 2- **limits**, contours and delimitations, 3- identification of **neighborhoods**, 4- **nodal points**, places of convergence such as squares, intersections, 5- **landmarks**, spatial reference points regardless of scale. These aspects would generate a mechanism for locating and selecting preferred locations, a personalized locating mind map of the city.

The mental maps in Lynch, as well as the processes of the construction of narratives by cartography, have points of convergence, as it is necessary to have a mental plan to carry out a cartographic representation. What differs is that the first selection are personal landmarks of usage in the city and the second is a planification that emerges through the focus of a question.

One of the ways of perceiving the tensions and disputes present in a territory is the realization of the representation of spaces and their connection with different groups of people, through the use of cartographies, for example. This is an interesting process to reveal through multiple languages, images that signify personal and group trajectories.

The cartographic methodology, *Narrative Landkarten*, a theoretical support developed by researchers at the University of Siegen, wich has among them Prof. Dr. Bernhard Johann Fichtner, from the *Sieger Zentrum für Sozialisations Lebenslauf und Biographie* group, was used in investigations by the University of Alanus and demonstrated the versatility of design to carry out research and connection with immigrant and refugee groups[1].

This method starts with the use of basic materials such as paper and pencil and a request to make the drawing that can be; draw your house, draw your path to school, draw the place you like most about your school, among other possibilities.

The request to carry out a cartography focuses on the main question that one wishes to investigate, or the one that can reveal more aspects of the interviewees lives.

[1] Immigrants and refugees in Germany are related to flows of people coming from territories with internal political conflicts or between countries in dispute for hegemony or borders, especially due to geography and history, countries in the Middle East and some African nations.

One of the examples of the use of the cartographic data collection method was used in a research with refugees, from the doctoral thesis by Antonia Scholz; Einflussfaktoren beider Zieistaatsusche von Asylbewerbern einer befragung, at the University of Alanus, under the guidance of Prof. Dr. Axel F. Mancini, the researcher followed a class for immigrants/refugees for 4 years, with young people who did not speak full German or English, which initially made it difficult to understand the real situation and the need for help for these young people.

In this example, the use of cartography was essential to understand the dilemmas and objective needs that these young people faced in this process, in particular the precariousness of living conditions, for example food security, general housing conditions, among other important issues that could be revealed .

Drawing as a universal language enabled the connection and perception of the daily life of those people who recently arrived in Germany, without a link, needing to establish relationships to get on with their lives and overcome their initial difficulties.

Another important example was carried out in Brazil with the use of cartographies in the research project – Dealing with new spaces: children and adolescents in the appropriation of the CEU Butantã architectural complex (São Paulo, Brazil), addressed the perception of students and teachers in relation to the CEU Butantã space.

In this case, the teachers' view revealed the pedagogical actions facing the challenges faced in everyday school life, their decisions, reflections and results in a process on the appropriation of spaces by students.

CEU Butantã is located in a neighborhood with great differences in living conditions, it has contrasts in relation to housing, on the one hand, on the side with higher topography, are the middle class houses and on the other side in the lower part, next to a polluted and unchanneled stream, there are precarious housing with risk of flooding, as shown in the images.

FIGURE 1. **CEU Butantã surroundings (stream)**

FIGURE 2. **CEU Butantã surroundings (lower part)**

FIGURE 3. CEU Butantã surroundings

FIGURE 4. CEU Butantã surroundings (high part)

One of the important issues of this public equipment is the coexistence and permeability offered to children and families who share the same privileged school space.

The attendance of children portrays the mosaic of the neighborhood, both middle-class children and poorer children, children of teachers and employees, coexist as students in this space, with a consolidated democratic proposal.

Teachers at the Municipal School of Early Childhood Education (EMEI), which is part of the CEU Butantã, carried out cartographies wich the intention was to identify their favorite places of activity. The material offered by the researchers was paper and graphite and colored pencils, colored pens, crayons and eraser.

The drawings were carried out in two stages and most of the teachers chose to use the graphite pencil. At first, it should only represent the space used in pedagogical practices, especially outdoors and toys that are regularly available.

In a second moment, it was requested that the first drawing be resumed, that the representations contained in it be observed. Next, a sheet of tracing paper was offered to overlay the first drawing and create a second layer, as this paper has a degree of transparency, it was asked that the teachers draw the children in these spaces and their actions in this new layer. At that moment, the researchers observed that the drawing gained movement and life, expressing feelings, desires and learnings.

After the steps of building the cartography using drawing as a medium, the teachers were asked to report their feelings when carrying out the cartography and what they perceived in the steps developed. The reports that followed showed how much movement the original drawing gained with the inclusion of children and that there was a concern on the part of teachers to represent each of their students, revealing that some of them were close to their favorite places, or their favorite toys.

A fact to note is that constructed spaces, however better and more generous they may be, gain a human dimension and the meaning inherent in this relationship in the presence of its fundamental actors, a school does not have its function recognized without the students, the teachers , managers, operational staff, without the presence of parents.

The cartographies revealed many feelings about the teaching work, the look on children and the most representative activities.

The choices made by the teachers revealed the concern for all the children, their preferences for places to develop activities, demonstrating an attentive look and the teacher's partner for each of their students.

FIGURE 5. **Teacher Cartography EMEI CEU Butantã**

Another fruitful example that was part of the same survey at CEU Butantã occurred at the CEI Child Education Center, where younger children are kept, who are generally exposed to pedagogical practices more focused on exploring the spaces offered at the CEU. Children move to different spaces daily, using most of the outdoor areas.

By having a very generous space, many games and activities are made so that children can experiment and develop their development skills and explore their creativity.

During the research, the CEI teachers decided to carry out their cartographies using photographs of various activities they carry out with the children and reveal the daily life of pedagogical actions in the appropriation of CEU spaces.

In a universe that uses images captured through cell phones, there is a challenge in thinking of the symbolic representation of the photographic image as a language with codes that are inherent to this technological apparatus. And it is necessary to consider what a photograph is.

It is worth mentioning that, even reproducing a situation, the image of people and actions cannot be considered reality, but it is a time frame, which according to Barthes would be; a look frozen in time and space.

FIGURE 6. **CEI CEU Butantã Cartography**

One of the fundamental aspects is the understanding of time and space in the representation of cartographies. This aspect can be understood by the chronotope concept, which alludes to a time of existence in a given space of a literary narrative.

According to Barbosa,

> (...) são esses espaços que carregam as marcas de um tempo pretérito para dentro do presente.
>
> *(...) these are spaces that carry the marks of a past time into the present. (Author's translation)*

Bakthin defines by;

> Aqui o tempo condensa-se, comprime-se, torna-se artisticamente visível; o próprio espaço intensifica-se, penetra no movimento do tempo, do enredo e da história. Os índices do tempo transparecem no espaço, e o espaço reveste-se de sentido e é medido com o tempo. Esse cruzamento de séries e a fusão de sinais caracterizam o cronotopo artístico. (Bakhtin, 2002: 211)
>
> *Here time condenses, compresses itself, becomes artistically visible; space itself intensifies, penetrates the movement of time, plot and history. The indexes of time transpire in space, and space takes on meaning and is measured with time. This crossing of series and the fusion of signs characterize the artistic chronotope. (Bakhtin, 2002:211)(Author's translation)*

In this case, the representation through narrative maps can be performed through different languages and reflect the relationship of space, time, memory, personal senses and their subjectivities.

Alfred Schütz's phenomenologically oriented sociology, and Peter L. Berger and Thomas Luckmann's constructivist sociology of knowledge is referenced in DREHER, 2011, which translates these interfaces as follows;

> De acordo com Berger e Luckmann, a legitimação da ordem social – de estruturas de poder inclusive – ocorre com o auxílio de totalidades simbólicas que, na vida cotidiana, sequer podem ser experimentadas – a ordem institucional se encontra integrada em um sistema relacional universal, de modo que cada experiência humana pode ser pensada como ocorrência no interior do universo simbólico legitimado. "O universo simbólico deve ser compreendido como matriz de todas as significações socialmente objetivadas e subjetivamente reais. Toda a história social e a biografia completa do

indivíduo são acontecimentos no interior deste universo" (ibidem, p. 114). Em sua forma objetiva, universos simbólicos correspondem a acúmulos de saber e, enquanto tais, a produtos sociais com uma história. (DREHER, p. 487)

According to Berger and Luckmann, the legitimation of the social order – including power structures – occurs with the help of symbolic totalities that, in everyday life, cannot even be experienced – the institutional order is found integrated in a universal relational system, of so that each human experience can be thought of as an occurrence within the legitimized symbolic universe. "The symbolic universe must be understood as the matrix of all socially objectified and subjectively real meanings. The entire social history and complete biography of the individual are events within this universe" (ibid., p. 114). In their objective form, symbolic universes correspond to accumulations of knowledge and, as such, to social products with a history. (DREHER, p. 487) (Author's translation)

Narrative maps as a biographical instrument present the relationship between people and their space and immediate surroundings, in a way, in the phenomenological approach, it reveals the tension between a palpable world and a potential, sensory world.

The narrative maps revealed by cartographies that use visual information present new concepts to be faced, we used Barthes (2005) to understand the visual information, looking for initial clues with questions such as;

"(...) a informação visual deve mobilizar disciplinas muito diversas, que frequentemente se ignoram mutuamente, (...)"

"(...) visual information must mobilize very different disciplines, which often ignore each other, (...)" (Author's translation)

This statement leads us to consider the meanings given to the images and the possible readings according to the particular universe of each interlocutor, however, the image must provoke the opening up to unanswered questions and therefore the potential for interdisciplinares that force the search for answers which cross multiple areas of knowledge and their codes. Above all, they challenge to think from another point of view.

The photographic image presupposes a cut of a moment and a context that one wants to produce a representation – in photography there is the freezing of the image in time, but the selection made by the photographer, however, there is no way to know the general context in which the image was produced. Barthes alludes to seeing the photograph of a king, which actually gives him the opportunity to observe the gaze of the king's photographer, frozen in time.

In his classic work The Clear Camera, Barthes will attribute two perspectives to the existence of photography, chemistry through the development process and physics, image formation through an optical apparatus linked to the subjective sphere of the selection made by the photographer's gaze in their relationship with the photographed subject or object and the spectator, who will be offered the experience of visualizing the record made, the photograph.

Contemporaneity displaces the development through chemical products for the materialization of the image through software, which has a new materiality, unknown by Barthes, who approached it until the advent of the polaroid camera with instantaneous development. For him there was the possibility of having fun with this apparatus, however, a dimension was subtracted, the tension existing in the process of developing the photograph.

In the case of narrative maps made with photographs, there is a selection of photographs to carry out a narrative about the question raised in the research, seeking to demonstrate the relationship between children in kindergarten and the space of CEU Butantã.

Every selection presupposes the choice of an image and the suppression of others, however, in an Era of profusion of images in exponential numbers, the choice is based on the motive and especially focuses on the viewer and the need to convey a message by image.

Thus, when carrying out the cartography, organizing the images and the connection between them, the kindergarten teachers used the resource of photographic images to translate how the children in their class, in view of the proposed pedagogical actions, triggered the appropriation of the CEU space.

The languages its codes cross and impact subjects in different situations, one of the potentials of the arts is to reach different perceptions according to cultural and social processes, worldview, reveals different possibilities of interpretation and provocation to a certain extent.

Dewey, explains what it means to have an experience,

> "A experiência ocorre continuamente, porque a interação do ser vivo com as condições ambientais está envolvida no próprio processo de viver. Nas situações de resistência e conflito, os aspectos e elementos do eu e do mundo implicados nessa interação modificam a experiência com emoções e ideias, de modo que emerge a intenção consciente."(DEWEY, 2012:109)
>
> *"The experience takes place continuously, because the interaction of the living being with environmental conditions is involved in the process of living itself. In situations of resistance and conflict, the aspects and elements of the self and the world involved in this interaction modify the experience with emotions and ideas, so that conscious intention emerges." (DEWEY, 2012:109)(Author's translation)*

The city as a field of disputes already evoked in this text, which in the face of an open code suits its interpreter, enables the reading of different layers of present meanings, especially when they gain a magnifying glass in the translation of particular perceptions.

Artistic productions and their interventions in the public space, of works designed from social issues in research and reflection groups, have been a front of many works by professor, researcher and plastic artist Bianka Mieskes of the University of Alanus, creating a counterpoint between academic research and intervention and artistic expression in cities.

The researcher presents one of her participations as a visual artist in the "Welcome " Project, which took place in Fortaleza in partnership with the Federal University of Espirito Santo and the change in the exhibition's objectives in light of the outbreak of a social fact in Brazil in 2017, as follows your presentation;

> "I planned a project entitled 'Culture under construction', but it turned out to be different: In February 2017, a police strike sparked a wave of violence. It was not predictable when the situation would stabilize. So there was only one possible topic "fragile – the thin skin of civilization."
>
> All interested artists and students were invited to participate. Recent events were critically reflected in an open and individual dialogue, artistic expressions were developed. Almost 50 students from Brazil, Germany, Norway and China participated in the project. Portuguese, German and

> English were spoken to. I tried to translate as much as possible, for ease of understanding, despite the language barrier. Here art creates the bridge easily. The exhibitions feature a range of paintings, sculptures, new media, actions in public space and performances. The exhibition is an experimental exercise in reflecting and questioning events. Positions are presented from shocking to poetic." (MIESKES, 2017)

The work shown below alludes to the number of deaths resulting from the civil police's strike and riots during the episode in Espírito Santo. The second work deals with the central issue of the exhibition, the fragile, thin skin of civilization.

It is worth reflecting on the invisibility of the imprisoned subjects, when signaling their bodies and the number of bodies that represent people, they gain visibility. It would also be worth saying who they were, for what they paid their sentences, their origin and how they were killed, by the other prisoners or by police repression.

In the face of the chaos and violent dynamics, exposing a new point of view that makes people think about facts in a less mediatic way, shifts the meaning and brings a new confrontation, of numbers that are not just figures, but bodies represented in the streets, bringing it to a new reality. In the same sense, the fragility of life, of existence, is present in the theme of the exhibition, which occupied an internal space in a gallery and the streets.

The record turns back to photography as a repository of ephemeral works of art, to maintain memory and history with possibilities of other languages that become a record of a fact, and can be used as foreseen by the new historiography, especially those arising from École des Annales, incorporates new documents and ways of inquiring facts, transforming them into new sources, into a historical document.

FIGURE 7. **Robin Hengesbach Urban Intervention in Plaster, How Much is 164?**

FIGURE 8. **Katharina Haupt, work in wood, What is the element that cannot be taken away from society?**

Invisibility is a theme that arises in academic research that has gained prominence in scientific journals, such as the FAPESP, it disseminates important research in the country, demonstrating the effects on immigrants, refugees, especially children and adolescents. In the research carried out by Fernanda Paraguassu, whose dissertation title, awarded by CAPES, is Narratives of refugee childhoods, children as protagonists of their own history. Invisibility condemns.

Studies of this nature reveal the daily life faced by children who take care of the home while their parents work to support everyone. In this sense, the school's attention and support are essential to keep children attending school, an important aspect for their social and future autonomy. Actions in schools should value the integration between cultures, approximation and understanding of the other to avoid discrimination, as shown by studies on the subject. There is a similarity in this example to the thesis carried out at the University of Alanus, which proves the urgency of awareness in the world.

Invisibility, whether due to poverty, restriction of freedom, to lack of knowledge and acceptance of cultural differences, whatever the reason, is harmful and perverse. Understanding each of the situations is necessary in order not to homogenize assessments, to place different subjects and situations in the same place, with the same answer. Human diversity accompanies the diversity of situations faced. Just as research has an increasing need to search for interdisciplinary answers, in the same way new questions provoke the displacement of old answers, it is necessary to face the contemporary dilemmas. It may be that we are moving towards understanding ourselves as human beings, multicultural, free from prejudice and empty ideological meanings. Hope is always worth hoping.

Bibliography

BAKHTIN, Mikhail. Questões de Literatura e Estética: a teoria do romance. 5ª ed. São Paulo: Annablume; 2002.

BARBOSA, Márcia Helena Saldanha, O Cronotopo e a Inserção da História na Narrativa de Dyonélio Machado. Available in: https://www.ufrgs.br/gthistoriaculturalrs/marcia_barbosa.html, Acess in:30 out.2021.

BARTHES, R. Inéditos vol. 3- imagem e moda, São Paulo, Ed. Martins Fontes, 2005. A Câmera Clara, Rio de Janeiro, Nova Fronteira, 2015.

DEWEY, j. Arte como experiência, São Paulo, Martins Fontes, 2012.

DREHER J. Fenomenologia do poder, Civitas Porto Alegre v. 11 n. 3 p. 474-490 set.-dez. 2011. Available in: file:///C:/Users/ihamb/OneDrive/Imagens/10061-Texto%20do%20artigo-36492-1-10-20111118.pdf. Acess in: 1 nov. 2021.

LYNCH, K. The Image of the City, Cambridge: M. I. T. Press, 1960.

MIESKES, B. PELED, Y. Gallary GAP, UFES, Vitória do Espirito Santo. - Brasil 19/04/2017 - 31/05/2017, catálogo.

ORLANDI, A.P. Sujeitos invisíveis, Pesquisa FAPESP, São Paulo, N308 (83-85) out 2021.

6. TRANSLATING CITY WALLS: SPACE AND SYMBOLIC POWER

Fernando de Oliveira Domingues Ladeira

Introduction

Cities [1]are not just the smallest autonomous administrative units, they maintain a symbolic relationship with their residents, a relationship that is established in feelings of love or hate with space.

Due to their walls and gates, sculptures and squares, cities communicate with their residents, their physical structures are silent, but not inert, they are expressions of power relations that confront, segment, unite, and surreptitiously, when one of these powers becomes superior, it shapes behavior and stabilizes society. However, this stabilization is precarious, as it aims to maintain the *status quo* and can be perceived in moments of social and ideological mutations when not absorbed by the dominant structure.

In cities, the relationship between morality and politics is established, as Plato states in The Republic (2019), because the good man can only be the good citizen, a just city is a city inhabited by just citizens and this was the Platonic project of the ideal city. The ideal city presents a social fabric stable and just, the analogy with the fabric indicates that notwithstanding being formed by different parts, it creates an indissoluble autonomous unit

[1] The title of city, in Brazil, was a purely honorific title. There was no administrative distinction in colonial Brazil between towns (village) and cities and it did not bring any privileges (Prado Junior, 2008, p. 304, note 08). From the royal act of recognition of a locality as a town (village), the municipal councils (legislative Power) could be installed, composed of two ordinary judges, serving one at a time, or the judge from outside and the three aldermen; were employees of the legislative Power the prosecutor, the treasurer and the clerk, all elected, like the ordinary judges and councilors, according to Victor Nunes Leal (2012, p. 76).

in which each part has a structural role in the set that becomes stronger than its parts. It is the city, therefore, the symbol of social cohesion, of the unification of distinct parts in a single weave, the unification of morality with politics.

St. Augustine takes up the idealized conception of the city, distinguishing the *Civitas Dei* from the *Civitas diaboli*. To be a citizen of City of God is to consider oneself a citizen of the cosmos, to be part of Nature, to be part of a whole, whereas in the City of Devil the aspects of individuality are accentuated, there is no idea of the notion of a whole. (MORA, 2004, p. 455).

Understanding cities requires translating their language, elucidating their symbols and their polysemic meanings. Excavating the surfaces of concrete in search of meaning in its structures enables a new vision for the origin of social conflicts and the violence that is exercised daily against countless individuals, symbolic violence, but not abstract, as concrete and painful as physical violence.

In cities, the first political conflicts arise between different conceptions of the world, that is, the conflicts take place between cultural institutions, no longer between individuals. Although it is still in the space of cities where these conflicts take place, because in them there is the smallest distance between the holders of symbolic power and the individuals.

Legal science has legal mechanisms to establish plans for the sustainable and socially fair development of cities, however, laws do not change reality, it is necessary to understand reality and so propose effective mechanisms to change the social situation.

The purpose, therefore, of this work is to outline the language of cities, to make explicit the existence of voices in their walls, to try to point out the existence of the silent voices of the permanent symbolic power that spreads through their streets, based on the symbolism that has always existed in the cities as reflections of the cosmos.

1. Cultural institutionalism, ideology and oppression

Social reality, as Marx said, quoted by Miaille (1979, p. 68), determines consciousness. Reality is a totality structured on three levels: at the base, the economic structure, the relations of production; at the second level, the legal and political systems; on the third level, ideology. The second and third levels are the so-called superstructures, but it is necessary to understand that this conception is holistic, that is, society is the totality of the three levels that cannot be separated and whose structuring is a working hypothesis.

As members of the superstructure, it is not the Law that exerts the effective repression, the sanction is actually the exception, as Miaille (1979, p. 85) points out, repression is the result of ideology, it is preexistent to the obligation established by Law, a silent, effective, and insidious repression that does not allow itself to be perceived.

Repression pre-exists the Law, in this conception it is the result of an invisible disciplinary power that is everywhere, within a structure of disciplinary micropowers that make "a relational power that is self-sustaining by its own mechanisms and replaces the brightness of manifestations by the uninterrupted game of calculating gazes" (FOUCAULT, 1997, p. 174).

This disciplinary mechanism is not exercised by means of penalizing sanctions, as the criminal system does with its prohibitive rules. Disciplinary power [2] is silent and is exercised through normalizing sanctions, not only separating what is forbidden from what is allowed, but also grading behaviors into good and bad ones. Everything is subjected to the normalizing sanction that classifies behaviors according to what ideology considers normal, good, acceptable and within what is acceptable, it still establishes degrees of optimal and sub-optimal; people are not treated as autonomous individuals, but objects to be subdued to classification, it is a matter, as Foucault says, "to penalize the most tenuous fractions of the conduct (...) that each individual is within a punishable-punishing universality" (FOUCAULT, 1997, p. 176).

The normalizing sanction underlies the Law, it acts in parallel, but in a system of "perpetual penalty" as it is present since childhood, and its "art of punishing" is not repression or expiation, but a "coercion of conformity to accomplish" (Foucault, 1997, p. 179).

Reality underlies the Law which, in turn, creates a whole stabilizing legal imaginary that only hides the true bases on which the normative edifice was built; in this sense, the Law consists of a language in which lies the 'ideological reserve'; it brings together men and objects in a single

[2] The disciplinary power in the conception of normalizing sanctioning power should not be confused with the disciplinary power of Administrative Law, this form of power falls within the broad sense of prohibitive rules.

language and establishes a global vision and, in order to stabilize the ideology, a whole set of norms, techniques and bureaucracy is structured to concretize the ideology (MIAILLE, 1979, pp. 91-93).

The structuring nature of an imaginary reality through Law avoids in-depth questioning about the very purpose of Law beyond the often--repeated fixed formulas of constitutional articles, because as Sérgio Buarque de Holanda (1995, p. 157) has already warned, Brazilians have a

> a pronounced love for fixed forms and generic laws, which circumscribe the complex and difficult reality within the scope of our desires, is one of the most constant and significant aspects of the character of Brazilians. [...] Everything that dispenses any refined and fatiguing mental work, the clear, lucid, definitive ideas, which favor a kind of atony of the intelligence, seem to us to constitute the true essence of wisdom. It is possible to understand the good success of positivism among us [...] precisely because of this rest that the irresistible and imperative definitions of Comte's system allow to the spirit.

Ideology refracts reality and without delving into the submerged layers of what is presented to us as the language of facts, it is not possible to know the essence of reality and understand one's own behaviors and attitudes.

Ideology should be understood as an 'imaginary relationship with the real' (MIAILLE, 1979, p. 46) is a stabilizing factor, because it is through it that individuals are convinced about established values, in this sense, without people being convinced of the importance of the State in the function of social appeasement, its operation would not be possible, and this is the function of Law: to establish notions such as general interest, rights and duties, sovereignty, defense, solidarity, "without which, after all, the functioning of the state institution would be compromised" (MIAILLE, 1979, p. 45).

It is up to the Law to promote imaginary reforms, as instruments for relieving social pressure, through the enactment of laws and regulations that appear to welcome social aspirations, when, in fact, effective solutions to social problems are not promoted by enacting laws, but by interventions in reality.

As Drummond (2006, p. 160) reminds us,

> Men ask for meat. Fire. Shoes.
> Laws are not enough. Lilies are not born
> of law. My name is turmoil, and it is written
> in stone.

In Brazil, the solutions to all problems are credited, by the political agents, and accepted by the citizens, to elections and enactment of new laws, for Brazilians, "the lilies are born of law" and this mentality ideologically constructed prevents the perception that the real change must be promoted through social pressures that require, however, overcoming ideological barriers. According to Buarque de Holanda (1995, p. 178),

> The reformers find only two solutions to the problems: replacement of the government leadership, which is a random remedy, and pretending to pace events according to systems, laws or regulations of proven virtue, in the belief that the dead letter can influence by itself and forcefully influence destiny of a people. The rigidity, the impermeability, the perfect homogeneity of legislation seems to us to be the only mandatory requirement of good social order. We ignore other resource. This truth escapes us that written laws, manufactured by jurisconsults, are not the most legitimate guarantees of happiness for people and stability for nations.

But ideology does not come only from Law, but is structured through various signs, whether linguistic or of another nature, such as through culture, music, sculpture and even the structure of cities, as Mario Quintana teaches us (2019),

> Only on the walls of the old cities
> hieroglyphs are drawn
> Only on the wall of lonely rooms,
> more than at Balthazar's feast,
> messages appear.
> You say it's from the humidity? Stop positivism!
> Humidity is a writing medium like any other.
> You, who only know the 23 or 25 letters of the alphabet,
> don't be so logical...Listen to the Poet's reading.

The walls speak to us, because the language is not only vocalized, it is in the intonation, in the gestures, in the symbols, in the walls, in the gates, in the social segregation, in the privatization of the public space.

Individuals are immersed in a set of codes that are established not only by Law, the regulation of social life is much more intense than that established by legal norms and much more effective as the regulation itself is established by the physical structures of the concrete structures of cities, or even the symbolic structure of culture that lay down oppression through opaque means, as Foucault (1997, p. 33) points out,

> The man we are told about and invited to release is already in himself the effect of a subjection much deeper than he. A 'soul' inhabits him and brings him into existence, which is itself a part of the domain exercised by power over the body. The soul, effect and instrument of a political anatomy; the soul prison of the body.

It is necessary to understand that the space of power dispute is exercised in a physical space, but this dispute changes from the understanding that the individual does not act in isolation, individuals are influenced by the ideology that shapes them and, therefore, the political dispute changes its figure to be configurated in disputes not of people, but of institutions, conceptions and in this perspective the analysis of the spaces of power dispute that develop in the space of coexistence of the individuals unfolds in an institutional way.

The traditional view of political conflict is exposed by Carl Schmitt as the dispute between friends and enemies, for this conception, politics is a conflicting relationship between groups and aims at domination, in this conception politics as mediation is not considered, because politics, although may result in pacification, it is not done by arbitrating plural interests, as politics is, in the words of Schmitt (2019, p. 57) the "most intensive and extreme opposition".

Within the institutionalist perspective, individuals act conformed by a set of regulations ranging from physical structural regulations, of streets, walls, to legal rules established by laws, rules of normalizing disciplinary power, the cultural rules of language, art, media and communication that are part of an ideology and that institutionalizes behaviors, hence the name to this conception of institutionalism that in the words of Nobel

Prize winner John Nörth, quoted by Pierson (2004, p. 165), are the "[R] rules of the game in a society or, more generally...the human constraints conceived and which shape human interaction".

The emphasis is no longer on the individuality and view of groups in the dispute for power, but on the institutional organization of the community, its power structures, and its mechanisms of distributing competencies as the main factor structuring behaviors.

For institutionalism, an institution is: "broadly speaking, the official and unofficial procedures, protocols, norms and conventions inherent to the organizational structure of the political community or political economy" (HALL and TAYLOR, 2003, p. 196), being part of this definition, the set of norms and conventions enacted.

One of the answers sought in the study of politics, under the institutional bias, is to analyze how institutions affect the behavior of individuals and according to the cultural, normative or discursive conception of institutionalism, institutions are defined by symbols, values and myths. It is a critical conception of the idea that institutions are a rational choice of individuals; within sociological institutionalism, emphasis is given to the fact that institutional practices, norms and bureaucracies are not the result of rationality, but of culture, like myths and ceremonies; these practices would then be incorporated into organizations. By this conception, the structure of an institution is dependent on what people believe.

Theorists of this school "tend to define institutions much more globally than political science researchers, including not only formal rules and procedures but also cognitive symbols and schemas and moral models" (HALL and TAYLOR, 2003, p. 209).

There is an interpenetration between institutions and culture and a tendency to define culture as institutions, a "cognitivist turn in the heart of Sociology" is inserted (HALL and TAYLOR, 2003, 209), which consists of moving away from conceptions that associate culture to norms, affective attitudes and values, to approach a conception that considers culture as a network of habits, symbols and scenarios that provide models of behavior.

The influence of institutions is not just about the ought, that is, about what I must do to avoid breaking the rules, but even influencing what I can imagine doing.

Symbols are built by institutions and are embedded in the individual's own shaping of the way he or she sees the world. Therefore, what may seem to a person a rational choice, has actually been constructed.

From this perspective, what gives "legitimacy" to certain institutional arrangements are "the sources of cultural authority" (HALL and TAYLOR, 2003, p. 212) which do not necessarily derive from political power, that is, from the State, but often from the media and economic power and currently from the big techs that are responsible for the intermediation of almost all discourses.

But how is this done?

This is done through stereotypes that create implicit meanings in signs that are accepted as normal when in fact they aim to justify or manipulate behaviors. This process is established by imperceptible social contexts. Thus, some design becomes a symbol from a social repertoire and context and for this reason its meaning cannot be understood without an immersion in the cultural values of the person who uses that symbol.

This entire process occurs in the individual experience, as individuals adapt and develop based on the differentiations and identifications they make since birth. Thus, for each element they add positive and negative values, in this sense, the light is identified with the mother's presence, with security, from the remote past of breastfeeding and the dark with fear, loneliness, the moment when the child wakes up only in the middle of the night (TUAN, 2015, p. 38).

We begin to attribute a positive value to light, and a negative value to darkness, arising from fear. These values can be ideologically manipulated to impose positive or negative values on other elements through association with light and dark. This is done through semantic corridors, isotopic rows, *videlicet*, in the mold of the dark that already had that negative value, other elements are inserted by force of manipulation to extend to another sign a negative connotation and so the issues of racial prejudice arise, by which a negative value is attributed by associating negative values to an attribute that had nothing in its origin with a negative value, it was a value attributed to a different object that through the semantic corridors magnetized another sign and thus racial prejudice is born.

This whole process of signification is what is called semiosis, which is defined by Isidoro Blikstein as a process of signification in which ideological traits trigger a whole configuration of "mold" or "semantic corridors" through which the fundamental lines of signification will flow, or rather, the isotopies of a community's culture, these semantic corridors that guide our perception of values, are "social glasses" (BLIKSTEIN, 2020, p. 187).

This conception gives great importance to the idea of ideology, for as Volóchnov (2017, p. 91) reminds us, everything that is ideological has meaning because it "represents and replaces something outside it". Where something represents something else, there is a process of differentiation and approximation, but this object not only reflects another reality, but it also refracts this reality, in other words, the signs do not transport us to the reality of the objects they represent without promoting some deformations of this same object.

Ideology is exercised by culture, understood as a set of symbols that create a representation of the world that is actually a second reality, created by power relations that are at the source of symbolic production, a system of domination; this representation established by culture plays a structuring role in reality and legitimizes domination regimes (MICELI, 2015, p. XV-XVI).

There is a system of domination that is exercised through the production and conservation of symbolic capital and its reproduction creates a continuous system, called by Pierre Bourdieu, the inculcation system "capable of producing agents endowed with a "secondary *habitus*, *that is,* a ethos and a secondary *eidos* that constitute the products of the internalization of a set, more or less integrated into a system, more or less extensive, more or less appropriate, of these schemes" structured within a system of circulation of symbolic goods established in a system of "monopoly of the legitimate exercise of symbolic violence" (BOURDIEU, 2015, p 118).

According to Pierre Bourdieu (2020, pp. 07-08), symbolic systems are not only structuring constituents, instruments of knowledge and construction of the world, as stated by neo-Kantian tradition of Durkheim, nor a structured system, as proposed by Sassure, who does not consider symbolic power essential in the construction of the world, but in the representation of structures, an intermediary. In Bourdieu's conception, symbolic powers are instruments of communication and knowledge, structured and structuring, and "fulfill their political function as instruments of imposition or legitimation of domination that contribute to ensuring the domination of one class over another" through "symbolic violence" and thus contributing to the domestication of the dominated" (BOURDIEU, 2020, pp. 07-08). Regulation is established through a "cultural law" (BOURDIEU, 2015, p. 209) in which the arbitrariness of this law is not recognized.

The feedback of the symbolic system is established within urban circles, through the segregation of social classes, given that the impediment of access to sources that produce symbolic power, such as the educational system, prevents the assimilation of cultural laws, in fact, the physical distance imposed between different social environments, peripheral neighborhoods, ends up preventing access to the dominant cultural law, in this sense, specific languages arise, circumscribed habits, distinct musical tastes that are not shared by the holders of the monopoly of symbolic violence, and with this an insurmountable obstacle of access to jobs, colleges, positions in the governance structure is established, making social mobility almost impossible. The inhabitants of the periphery become foreigners in their own country.

In other words, the best-paying jobs become accessible only to those who are able to speak, behave and dress according to social codes and do so unconsciously and without specific effort, while those who live in peripheral environments did not inculcate the dominant cultural rules, thus feeding inequality backwards, since knowing the dominant cultural codes is a prerequisite for access to the best social positions.

2. Symbolic power and(in) space

Symbolic power is exercised as a process, since it is mutable. It structures specific language system for fields of knowledge and, at the same time, it creates patterns of behavior, "a continuous crystallization of different types of norms, organizations and frameworks that regulate the processes of social exchanges" (SANTAELLA, 2018, p. 168).

From an ontological point of view, within Peirce's theory of categories, signs are classified from the point of view of quality (firstness) as a mere feeling, an existent (secondness) as a reaction or resistance, or a mediation (thirdness) as behavior regulation. But in all categories, the others are present, what exists is the prominence of one over the others (SANTAELLA, 2018, p. 170-171).

In the words of Barbosa da Silveira (2007, p. 42),

> Firstness, as its name implies, is the primary basis of all reality, being presupposed in existential confrontations, as well as in every continuum and in every generalization. Secondness, on the other hand, while presupposing firstness and constituting itself from it, maintains an irreducible specificity in relation to the former to the former. It, indeed, is characterized by the connection of two elements, not as mere potentials, but as mutually confronting, negating and limiting each other. Existing is, for Peircean theory, matters to others, in a theater of multiple reactions. Thirdness presupposes Secondness, and consequently, Firstness, allowing, however, that the update contained in the existential confrontation is generalized to third elements that do not directly maintain a relationship of action and reaction between themselves.

Institutions are signs of the order of Thirdness, as they govern, shape behaviors, but they also have the other categories and under the aspect of Firstness they are of the order of feeling that unite individuals, create a social image, such as the consideration they receive from society, and Secondness is their social role, their existent, their effective function (SANTAELLA, 2018, p. 170-171).

This semiotic process does not take place in the abstract, but in *locus*, there is a framed circumscription where semiotic practices of institutional scope are inserted and, in this scope natural and cultural aspects converge and acquire forms.

According to Milton Santos (2020, p. 12), space is the set of things – geographic, natural and artificial objects – plus society. Therefore, space is not just a set of material things, geographic objects, the cartography of city streets, it is all that, plus the social aspect of human activities and their institutional conformations, therefore, in the institutional sphere, they insert processes that are configured in functions, a destination to an end, and these functions result in forms that end up acquiring a territorial expression.

If, in Peirce's conception, all material and immaterial aspects configure signs, then social space constitutes a set of signs in a semiotic process, destined for an end and that are concretized in a form endowed with value and ideological content.

This semiotic process is done in relational iteration with individual values and physical and socio-environmental aspects that result in the differences that can be observed from clippings between different spaces, even if they originate from identical processes or from the same source. For being result of continuous processes, forms, forms are not static, they are mutable, which is why locations change, as they are bundles of social forces exerted in an area; a location excluded from the social is just a place (SANTOS, 2020, p. 13).

As Paul Claval explains,

> space is one of the privileged supports of symbolic activity. It is perceived and valued differently by those who inhabit it or value it [...]. Space thus lives in the form of mental images [...] The facts of power have a spatial dimension that relates to the elements embodied by them (CLAVAL, 1979, p. 20).

According to Milton Santos (2020, p. 19), the elements of space are men, firms, institutions, ecological support, infrastructures, but within the sociological conception of institution mentioned, it is possible to reduce these elements to three: institutions (including men, firms, ideologies); ecological support and infrastructure. From the variation of these elements, spaces are altered; in the same way, the variation in the valuation of each of these elements modifies the relationship of the individual with that of space, *v.g,* if a given society considers educational institutions important, then museums, schools result in greater valuation of space, even if the others variables are the same; however, if greater emphasis is placed on economic production, greater value will be given to infrastructure and, therefore, a space better served by this element will be more valued.

Hence, for Milton Santos (2020, p. 37), it is not possible to have a "valid interpretation of local systems at a local scale", which means that the interpretation of a space is linked to the set of ideological influences and the hue of the economic production of an epoch.

This dialectical relationship between the elements that make up the space, the variation in the valuation of each of the elements is the result of external influences. This means that spaces are in constant evolution and at each transition period there is a process of deculturalization, as there is a loss of ancestral references in a place that is no longer recognizable, either by migration, due to the inability of traditional populations to adapt to the new times, either by the entry of new inhabitants more suited to the new social conjuncture.

This occurs because within semiotics a thing does not have an intrinsic meaning, it is something because it is different from something else, therefore, it is in alterity that any element acquires a meaning, this also happens with individuals, the first perception of oneself is the difference from others, but in the search for identity, people do not see themselves only as different, but as different with something else that makes me unique and perhaps, deep down, this something else unveiled is something also shared by others and from there comes the possibility of all social magnetism, in the sense presented by Landowski (2012, p. 27).

The opposite effect also exists, because if I lose my something else, the intimate element of union with the whole, I lose my own identity and this process of disjunction occurs in deculturalization, that is, the loss of references from a displacement of place. Once identity is lost, all possibility of considering a point in common with humanity is lost, and from there on, there is only the other as a disjunctive element, as the different.

For Milton Santos (2020, p. 67),

> space constitutes an objective reality, a social product in a permanent process of transformation. Space imposes its own reality; that is why society cannot operate outside it [...] whenever society (the social totality) undergoes changes, forms or objects assume new functions; the totality of mutation creates a new spatial organization.

Space is not only in semiosis with the signs, the space itself is a sign because it has a meaning, because each person relates to a space in a different way, with feelings of belonging or strangeness and that generate deep bonds in different dimensions varying from a hometown, to a region or country, and this affective bond of a human being with a specific location was called by Tuan (2015, p. 113) as "topophilia". The relationship of men with cities is not an economic relationship, but an affective one.

Cities play a very prominent symbolic role and this semiotic configuration of cities dates back to their historical origin, as Tuan emphasizes (2015, pp. 175-176),

> When the study of urbanism goes back to its primitive centers and into the distant past, we do not find the market or the fortress, but the idea of the supernatural creation of the world. The agent is a god, a priest-king, or a hero: the locus of creation is the center of the world. This center is usually marked in some way. Perhaps starting as a tribal sanctuary, transforming into a compact and extensive ceremonial ensemble that includes different combinations of architectural elements such as platforms, terraces, temples, palaces, courtyards, stairs and pyramids. The city transcends the uncertainties of life; it reflects the accuracy, order and prediction of the heavens. Before writing was widespread, the world view was maintained by oral tradition, ritual and (not least) the semiotic force of architecture. Life can be more demanding in an ancient city than in a Neolithic village; but between the rites and the architectural splendor, a man, in the city, however humble, has something that the villager does not have — participation in the magnificence of a much larger world.

Cities originated from ritual meetings in specific places and, therefore, their origin is symbolic and from there comes the geometric shapes that aimed to reproduce the specific two-dimensional conception of the cosmos and were, in the words of Tuan, *Civitas Dei* on earth and as symbols of heaven in the earth they adopted circular, square or rectangular shapes and incorporated ziggurats, pillars and domes to enhance their vertical aspect and "reinforce the transcendental character of the city" (TUAN, 2015, p. 177-194).

In Brazil, the village, which were the administrative units of colonial Brazil and which were distinguished from the cities only by the honorific title, had in the pillories the symbol of the legal core, a symbol of royal authority and which served to bind criminals and disobedients; with the pillory were installed the customs and church, symbols of subordination to the king and the Church, "in the clear open in the forest, the pillory demonstrates that the king exists and is present" (FAORO, 2008, p. 178).[3]

[3] The cities in colonial Brazil were created by the royal authority, it was not a later act of recognition of an autonomous urban development, this is a mark of current mentality of using the Law to create reality, instead of using the Law only to regulate the reality. Campos and Parati stand out in colonial Brazil in which the residents raised their pillories awaiting the recognition of the royal authority. (FAORO, 2018, p. 173).

The symbolic and transcendental character of cities is present in their reference as a national symbol, usually being their capital, or, in the case of Brazil, Rio de Janeiro as a symbol and expression of 'brazilianness'.

The Brazilian capital Brasília has cosmic references, as Tuan (2015, p. 197) points out, mentioning Meira Penna, since its location, from the point of view of Dom João Bosco, in the nineteenth century, and its spatial symbolism indicates the rupture of land barriers to the interior of the continent to spread a sense of unity in the vast expanse of territory. Its design by Lucio Costa also has the shape of a cross, and reminds Tuan that it is an ancient tradition of dividing the land by two intersecting lines, indicating cardinal directions, besides being a reference to the Portuguese colonizers of erecting crosses when taking possession of lands, indicating that "Christ, the Kosmokrator, conquered chaos" (Tuan, 2015, p. 198). As one of the axes is curved it resembles a bird, so it would be "a bird that landed on earth, a new Jerusalem coming down from the heavens of God. In Jung's psychology, the bird is also a symbol of salvation, a sign of spiritualization" (Tuan, 2015, p. 198). Niemeyer's cathedral is a symbol of transcendence,

> a structure that rises on sixteen paraboloid buttresses that support the transparent roof. In order to enter it, the devotee must first cross the interior of the earth and pass, symbolically, through "the valley of the shadow of death". Inside, he is suddenly illuminated from the outside: his eyes are led by the ripple to the source of light and blessing (Tuan, 2015, pp. 198-199).

In the city of São Paulo, nowadays, the first reference is Paulista avenue, its location at a high point of the city gives it an aspect of prominence. The different phases it has gone through have always given this avenue the symbol of the dominant economic power of the respective historical period, before agriculture, today the financial conglomerates, and even though there has been a displacement of business centers to other regions, such as Faria Lima avenue, Paulista avenue has not lost the meaning of the economic strength of the State of São Paulo, but alongside this symbolism, one can also observe the symbols of two other powers parallel to the economic and equally responsible for the diffusion of the ideology, such as the antennas on the buildings that refer to the power of communication and also the São Paulo Art Museum (MASP) which is the symbol of art diffusion.

The reference to art is paradoxical, as art frees, but also enslaves, as it can be used for purposes other than those for which it was originally conceived. It is not art that liberates, it is the aesthetic gaze, which means that under the pressure of ideology, art is also a very effective instrument of ideological conformation, especially because art is an element of immediate consciousness, as it does not depend on codes and is capable of conviction through assent, a pure feeling.

The meaning of a work of art is also influenced by other elements arising from the text in which it is inserted, the text being understood as any environment in which a speech takes place in verbal language, gestural or through clothing and all other social codes.

In these terms, the statue of Borba Gato is a symbol in the city of São Paulo and its purpose is to be a reference to the pioneering nature of the people of São Paulo who, through the "Bandeirantes"[4], allowed the integration of the national territory and made possible the construction of a continental country, avoiding its segregation, this statue has a military bearing to indicate strength, and all elements that aim to infuse a conception, a historical representation, only through the force of symbolic power can achieve these references. Only through intertextual references is it possible to arrive at this conception of the pioneers as a symbol of strength, as an element of territorial integration, liberation from the oppression of the jungle and the savages.

However, intertextuality is ambivalent, because in the case of a symbol whose meaning is constructed by many linguistic, educational and social elements, it becomes polysemic, that is, with different meanings due to specific intertextual influences of the interpreter.

The generative path of meaning in Borba Gato's sculpture can only be understood through intertextuality with culture and, in this sense, it represents the role of liberator from the oppressions of the jungle and the unknown, the path therefore is oppression (jungle) → no freedom → freedom (civilization).

[4] The "Bandeirantes", also called "Sertanistas", were the pioneer explorers to explore the Brazilian territory, between the 16th and 18th centuries. They were responsible for expanding and conquering the limits of the Lusitanian colony's possessions.

However, if there is an awakening of ideological oppression, the reading can be in the opposite direction, recognizing in civilization an element of oppression and the natural state of the jungle as freedom: reading would then be freedom (jungle) → non-oppression → oppression (civilization), thus unveiling the ideological role of the figure of the pioneers (bandeirantes) as liberators and pointing out the oppressive role represented by the internalization of European civilization and culture for indigenous populations.

Therefore, depending on the personal circumstances of an individual, the symbolism of a statue or a work of art, or of a word or gesture, takes on different meanings. The interpretation of signs is ideological, except in Peircean firstness (2017) which, as pure feeling, assumes the character of ultimate interpretant.

The afore mentioned sculpture can be considered a symbol of oppression outside the ideological discourse. Within a plural democratic conception, different forms of expression of any worldview are required in cities, and if any work of art causes discomfort, it is an indication that ideological forces are acting and this moment becomes opportune to an introspection on one's own individual worldview with its prejudices.

The complexity of the theme increases when the city itself assumes an oppressive meaning, because if on the one hand it can generate positive feelings, the opposite can occur, in this context, neighborhoods marked by bars, gates acquire a meaning far beyond a public safety problem, but an excluding aspect for people outside of that specific group that is there.

As mentioned at the beginning, the walls speak if they are read in a non-positivist way, their stains are not just moisture, they are marks of an oppressive past, marks of inequality, marks of a deepening social segmentation, marks of a growing fear of the other, of the different.

Conclusion

Individuals perceive the world influenced by a set of external values and construct the meaning of cities from their signifying structures in flux.

Oppression is established far beyond physical restraint, because it is through symbolic power that domination is stabilized, conforming even the limits of the imaginary, confronting the discourse of freedom, because being free demands freedom from ideological chains.

Cities are the spatial units of symbolic power. As space, and not just place, they are symbols. Through their walls, walls, railings and avenues they are discoursing and the meaning that comes from their codes affects each person differently, based on their own values built in and by history, which explains the feelings of belonging and exclusion and their correlates of love and hate.

Raising ideological blindfolds is a prerequisite for planning plural spaces that dialogue with all individuals, as ideologies can only be confronted from the dissemination of different ideas, and this requires making public places effective public spaces.

Bibliography

ANDRADE, Carlos Drummond de. Antologia poética (organizada pelo autor). 58ª ed. Rio de Janeiro: 2006.

BLIKSTEIN, Izidoro. Semiótica e totalitarismo. São Paulo: Contexto, 2020.

BOURDIEU, Pierre. A economia das trocas simbólicas. 8ª ed. São Paulo: Perspectiva, 2015.

BOURDIEU, Pierre. O Poder Simbólico. São Paulo: Edições 70, 2020.

CLAVAL, Paul. Espaço e poder. Rio de Janeiro: Zahar Editores, 1979.

FAORO. Raymundo. Os donos do poder. Formação do patronato político brasileiro. 4ª ed. São Paulo: Globo, 2008.

FOUCAULT, Michel. Vigiar e Punir: nascimento da prisão. Tradução Raquel Ramalhete. 42ª ed. Petrópolis, RJ: 2014.

HALL, Peter A. TAYLOR, Rosemary. As três versões do neo-institucionalismo. Lua Nova nº 58, 2003.

HOLANDA, Sérgio Buarque de. Raízes do Brasil. 26ª ed., São Paulo: Companhia das Letras, 1995.

LANDOWSKI. Eric. Presenças do outro (E. 183). São Paulo: Perspectiva, 2012.

LEAL, Victor Nunes. Coronelismo, enxada e voto. O município e o regime representativo no Brasil. 7 ed. São Paulo: Companhia das letras, 2012.

MICELI. Sérgio. A força do Sentido. In. Economia das trocas simbólicas, p. VII-LXI. São Paulo: Perspectiva, 2015.

MORA, J. Ferrater. Dicionário de Filosofia. Tomo I. São Paulo: Loyola, 2004.

PEIRCE. Charles S. Semiótica. São Paulo: Perspectiva, 2017.

PIERSON, Paul. Politics in Time. Princeton University Press (Edição do Kindle), 2004.

PLATÃO. Box Grandes Obras de Platão. N.c.: Mimética (Edição do Kindle), 2019.

PRADO JUNIOR, Caio. Formação do Brasil contemporâneo: colônia. São Paulo: Brasiliense, 2008.

QUINTANA Mario. A vaca e o hipogrifo. Rio de Janeiro: MEDIAfashion, 2008, p. 217.

TUAN, Yi-Fu. Topofilia. Londrina: EDUEL (Edição do Kindle), 2015.

SANTAELLA, Lucia. Semiótica Aplicada. São Paulo: Cengage Learning, 2018.

SANTOS, Milton. Espaço e Método. 5ª ed. São Paulo: Editora da Universidade de São Paulo. 2020.

SCHIMITT, Carl. O conceito do político. Tradução: Alexandre Franco de Sá. Lisboa: Edições 70, 2019.

WEBER, Max. Economia y sociedade. 2ª ed. México: FCE, 2008.

7. DYNAMICS OF PERIPHERY IN SÃO PAULO: REFLECTIONS ON POSSIBLE PATHWAYS PROGRESSING TOWARDS SOCIAL RESILIENCE

Carlos Leite
Angélica Tanus Benatti Alvim
Jörg Schröder
Andresa Ledo Marques
Daniela Getlinger

1. Introduction: the context

The accelerated urbanization that occurred during the 20th century has left more than a billion people living in marginalized and fragile urban areas around the world, mostly within informal settlements and slums of developing nations. In the first decades of the 21st century, the picture is even bleaker, under the threats of the potential adverse impacts of climate change and, more recently, the devastating impacts of the Covid-19 pandemic.

The focus on critical urban situations, as brought forward with this article, involves a trans-scalar perspective on processes of spatial fragility and social inequality that affect not only specific areas, but are a danger for the future of entire urban systems, urban life, and urban economy. Effectively, the concept of peripheries as manifestation of marginalization – as shown in recent research (Schröder et al. 2018) – can be set in a transversal perspective across different contexts (metropolitan, intermediate, rural), in order to discover possibilities to transfer concepts and approaches; but also in a dynamic sense of changing interaction and linkages between different innovative spatial and social phenomena, that can not only be understood as enhancing force for overall systemic resilience, but that offer relevant potentials for local sustainable development.

Although the fragile peripheries contain active communities capable of restarting interaction, a future transition from the dangerous state of the fragmented metropolis to a state of dynamic territories that are progressing toward resilience will be necessary. Policies, projects, and actions can reactivate the possibilities and energy of the peripheries to increase the dynamism of a new development model – energies of people, places, nature, and ideas. Both concepts lead to a vision of peripheries as New Habitat – places of life, work, and culture – overcoming fragility and temporality in informal settlement and recognizing its value as a form of social and spatial intelligence that can become seeds for the overall resilience of metropolitan systems.

As an outcome of the cooperation between researchers from Mackenzie Presbyterian University (Brazil) and Leibniz Universität Hannover (Germany), the article is structured in four parts, besides the introduction and conclusion: the first part addresses a discussion on the role of peripheries in fostering a state of dynamic territories towards resilience, followed by the presentation of methodological paths for the construction *of new urban governance processes,* centred on action-oriented projects, place-based approach, and in-transition processes. The third part presents a brief overview of the peripheral and socially vulnerable areas in São Paulo. Finally, the fourth part of the article brings some reflections on urban experiences in Latin America that seek to promote the transformation of urban peripheries through new forms of urban governance and the valorization of the local scale.

2. Dynamics of peripheries: progressing towards social resilience

The increase in socio-spatial inequalities in many cities around the world, fostered by the near and longer term social and economic impacts of Covid –19, is becoming a major topic in scientific debate, e.g., in a geographical (Rose-Redwood, 2020) and economical perspectives (Blundell et al., 2020). Urban planning can be seen in a promising position to contribute to the evolving research in this context (Leite et. al., 2020), not only through novel empiric evidence of the comprehensive access to urban life and urban space in concrete situations, but also by means of innovative methodologies in a project – and development –oriented approach of "activist researchers" (Scaffidi et al., 2019).

In particular, a "territorial" notion of targeted urban planning projects in scale of neighborhoods not only extends to multiscale implications in urban networks but approaches challenges of climate change and social fragmentation with a "cosmopolitan mission" (Schröder et al., 2021), leading to a reformulation of concepts, models, and tools for urban transition to sustainability: (1) ecological transition to face climate change, "which refers to the process by which humans incorporate nature into society" (Bennett & Belshaw, 1976) and urban planning and design adaptation as a social and spatial process; and (2) a sustainable and inclusive transformation that includes social, cultural, spatial, ecological, and economic aspects and their interrelation.

Effectively, sectorial transition processes (in energy, industry, or agri-food) as well as mitigation and adaptation to hazards and changed nature in climate change are increasingly seen as deeply interconnected with social inclusiveness and collaboration to become effective as well as ethical (e.g., in the policy framework of the European Green Deal)([1]). In the comprehensive vision of urbanism, fragility as spatial manifestation of division and impact of nature, thus, is to be tackled not only in an ecological and social dimension, but overall, as a risk for cities as a living space.

As Henri Lefebvre (1967) put it, "the right to the city manifests itself as (...) right to habitat": thus, not only the important provision of basic services and safety, but the crucial possibility to participate and collaborate, that facilitate a right to the future. Still, the share of urban population living in informal settlements and slums – marginalized and fragile urban areas – counts to one billion([2]) and is constituting a major challenge for sustainability goals, first-hand UNSDG([3]) 11, to make cities and human settlements inclusive, safe, resilient, and sustainable.

[1] Available at: http://ec.europa.eu/info/strategy/priorities-2019-2024/european-green-deal_en

[2] Available at: http://www.un.org/sustainabledevelopment/cities/

[3] United Nations Sustainable Development Goals (UNSDG) is the 2030 Agenda for Sustainable Development composed by 17 objectives that were adopted by all United Nations Member States in 2015. More information is available at: https://sdgs.un.org/goals.

The focus on critical urban situations, as brought forward with this article, involves a trans-scalar perspective on processes of spatial fragility and social inequality that affect not only specific areas, but are a danger for the future of entire urban systems, urban life, and urban economy. Effectively, the concept of peripheries as manifestation of marginalization can be set in a transversal perspective across different contexts (metropolitan, intermediate, rural), in order to discover possibilities to transfer concepts and approaches; but also, in a dynamic sense of changing interaction and linkages between different innovative spatial and social phenomena that offer relevant potentials for local sustainable development (Schröder et al. 2018).

The concept of Territorial creativity, in a transdisciplinary range of formerly separated fields of urbanistic and other research and practice, highlights mechanisms to activate spatial and social capital that is neglected in mainstream urban and territorial development: extraordinary cultural resources as well as abilities in interactions between humans and environment that can bring high economic, social, and ecological benefit for all—if activated and supported by novel projects and new policies. This creativity of activation, a better use of local resources and goods (Moulaert et al., 2005), can serve as a basis for community building, social entrepreneurship, and cultural inventions which contribute to an ecological and social transition.

The concept of Reserves of Resilience highlights the possible reactivation of urban metabolisms in extended systems that, more and more, resemble archipelagos and matrices of places rather than satellite systems. Even if fragile peripheries contain active communities that are capable of restarting interaction, it will be necessary in the future to pass from the dangerous state of a fragmented metropolis to a state of dynamic neighborhoods that are in progress towards resilience. Policies, projects, and actions can reactivate the possibilities and energy of peripheries to enhance the dynamism of a new development model – energies of people, places, nature, and ideas. Both concepts lead to a vision of peripheries as New Habitat – places of living, work, and culture – surpassing fragility and temporality in informal settlement and recognizing its value as a form of social and spatial intelligence that can become seeds for the overall resilience of metropolitan systems.

3. Towards new forms of local urban governance

The seeds for resilience can be found and nurtured in marginal and fragile situations. Such seeds can be understood through Sennett's (2018) concept of liminal space which exists at the borders of standard cultural and political perception: porosity and borders "create liminal space; that is, space at the limits of control, limits which permit the appearance of things, acts, and persons unforeseen, yet focused and sited". In opposition to the attributes of closed systems – fixed shape, equilibrium, and integration – he characterizes liminal space even as crucial for an open system as non-linear, and within that frame range from path-dependency to the patterns of chance, in interaction between spatial creation and social behavior that together form urban agency/initiative. Liminal space thus can become a place and a disseminator for innovation towards resilience – in many fields of community and knowledge building for urban action e.g., for public space, water facilities, new models of social housing, use of renewable resources, sustainable mobility, new living-working models, circular economy, food cycles, etc. For this new urban governance initiative, three methodological and topical research avenues can be described:

Action-oriented projects: urban governance initiative needs narratives as analytical tool, in order to grasp cultural resources; but relies also on narratives as a projective tool implying a critique of scripts and indicators that lead to an "over-determination both of the city's forms and its social functions" (Matthey, 2014). Thus, narrative can be seen as a basis for action-oriented projects that are necessary as guidance to implement public policies effectively. Not only, but in peculiar form, trans-sectorial cooperation – within concrete and comprehensive urban projects – is crucial for interventions in fragile territorial contexts, converging different public policies and diverse civic initiatives, in social housing, public space and facilities, water sanitation, environmental risk protection, poverty, health, mobility, education, etc.

Place-based approach: in extension, for urban governance initiative, a place-based approach gives analytical access to specific forms of spatial and social capital, and foremost to their potentialities in a specific context, leading to place-based strategies that "consider economic, social, political, and institutional diversity in order to maximize both the local and the aggregate potential" (Barca; McCann; Rodriguez-Pose, 2012); as well as giving feedback for the further development of the – necessary and facilitating – policy frameworks, since in a place-based perspective "development intervention should increasingly focus on efficiency and social inclusion" (Barca; McCann; Rodriguez-Pose, 2012).

In-transition processes: urban governance initiative needs to be built on the interaction between bottom-up initiatives and associative networks – as strong points of true urban regeneration projects – directing frameworks, policies and public intervention, that facilitate to extend projects into processes of change: "Collaborative networks, advanced models of city-making, and social innovation initiatives are expressed in a rediscovered adaptive capacity of urban communities and, as a sort of 'local resilience', involved in bridging the dramatic gap of public welfare by offering a view of sharing and circularity..." (Lino 2018). Thus, public stakeholders, civic organizations, and economic actors need to develop coherent activities in form of a "third mission" as common engagement.

4. Dynamics of peripheries in Brazilian cities and São Paulo in 2020

Similar to other countries in Latin-America, Brazil Brazil has undergone an intense urbanization process since the late 20th century on, mostly due to intense internal migration from North-eastern Brazil towards the South--eastern region of the country. In the largest cities, those who migrated in search of jobs in the industrial sector started to occupy vacant land in the cities' outskirts, building their own houses mostly within illegal settlements and slums, due to insufficient social housing policies.

In 1940, 18.8 million people lived in cities in Brazil, accounting for 26.3% of the country's total population. In 2010, the census registered 84.35% of the country's total population living in urban areas (161 million inhabitants). In 70 years, about 142 million people have moved to urban settlements within Brazilian cities, most of them living in self-built houses without any funding or support from public policies (IBGE, 2010).

The gradual introduction of public facilities and services has benefited various territories located on the outskirts of cities, leading to a progressive improvement in the living conditions of the resident population. These changes were driven by the ongoing efforts of social movements that fought for urban reform. However, in the face of the urban crisis experienced in the early 21st century, it becomes evident that social inequalities within Brazilian cities have worsened. This deterioration occurred despite public investments, the expansion of participatory processes, and the diversity of urban development in the peripheries of cities. The complexity of the situation suggests that although significant progress has been made in some aspects, there are still substantial challenges to be overcome in order to achieve broader social and spatial justice in urban areas.

The IBGE (Brazilian Institute of Geography and Statistics) Demographic Census of 2010([4]) showed an unprecedented growth of slum areas in Brazil, emerging as one of the most relevant indicators of the dire urban situation in Brazil. The number of Brazilians living under such conditions rose from 6.5 million people in 2000 to 11.4 million in 2010 (Pasternak and D'Ottaviano, 2016).

Although slums are found in all regions of the Brazilian territory, they present a higher proportion in the Southeast Region, predominantly in large cities([5]) and since the 2000s also in medium-sized cities([6]). Pasternak and D'Ottaviano (2016) indicate, based on 2010 Census data, that of the 6,329 existing slums in the country, 3,954 were concentrated in the Southeast Region, which is home to the two largest Brazilian cities: São Paulo and Rio de Janeiro. The authors also point out that the Metropolitan Region of São Paulo (RMSP)([7]) has the highest number of slums in Brazil, concentrating 27% of all Brazilian slums in its territory.

The percentage of the population living in slums within the Metropolitan Region of São Paulo (RMSP), Brazil's main metropolitan area, increased from 8.14% of the region's total population in 2000 to 9.79% in 2010. By 2010, slums were recorded in 24 out of the 39 municipalities, amounting

[4] The preliminary version of the 2022 Census has not yet reported data on slums. In this article, we decided to use the 2010 Census as it includes detailed data on slums, enabling a more accurate analysis. It's significant to point out that the preliminary 2019 IBGE data on slums indicate that the share of households in slums reached 7.82% of the total housing units that year, accounting for more than 5 million slum households across the country, with an estimated population of nearly 20 million inhabitants (Pasternak and Bogus 2022). Such data is expected to be refined by the 2022 Census.

[5] According to IBGE, large cities are those with more than 500,000 inhabitants.

[6] According to IBGE, medium-sized cities are those with between 100,000 and 500,000 inhabitants.

[7] The Metropolitan Region of São Paulo is composed by 39 municipalities and is configured as one of the largest urban agglomerations in the world, concentrating in 2010 19,683,975 million inhabitants (IBGE, 2010).

to a total of 1,703 slums and more than 596,000 households (Pasternak and D'Ottaviano, 2016).

The distribution of slum-dwellers is predominantly peripheral. In the case of the city of São Paulo the largest proportion of this population has resided in the exterior ring and peripheral ring for many decades, as illustrated in Table 1 below.

TABLE 1: **Municipality of São Paulo – Proportion of slum-dwellers in the total population, 1991 to 2010, by rings.**

Ring	Proportion of slum-dwellers in the total population (%)			
	1991	1996	2000	2010
Central	0,05	0,05	0,00	0,00
Interior	0,90	0,90	0,78	0,10
Intermediate	5,24	5,24	7,19	5,62
Exterior	7,06	7,06	6,67	10,06
Peripheral	10,32	10,32	12,44	15,74
Municipality of São Paulo	7,40	7,40	8,94	11,38

Source: adapted from PASTERNAK, Suzana; D'OTTAVIANO, Camila, 2016.

Since 2012, the Rede Nossa São Paulo([8]) (RNSP) has been developing the Map of Inequality, a study based on official public data that concentrates annual indicators from 96 districts of the city of São Paulo. In their most recent review, in 2019, the indicators related to the territories of vulnerability corroborate the scenario placed under the data from the official 2010 census surveyed previously. The following map shows the proportion of households in slums in relation to the total number of households; with only 11 districts in the city without slums. The district with the highest incidence, Vila Andrade, has a share of 49,2%, while the average for the whole city is around 8,3% (RNSP, 2019).

[8] Rede Nossa São Paulo (RNSP) is a civil society organization founded in 2007. The organization involves different social actors and aims at promoting and building an agenda that supports the public sector in the formulation of more inclusive, sustainable, and transparent policies.

FIGURE 1. **Map of Inequality showing the proportion of slums in the total number of households, by district. Vila Andrade presents the highest incidence.**

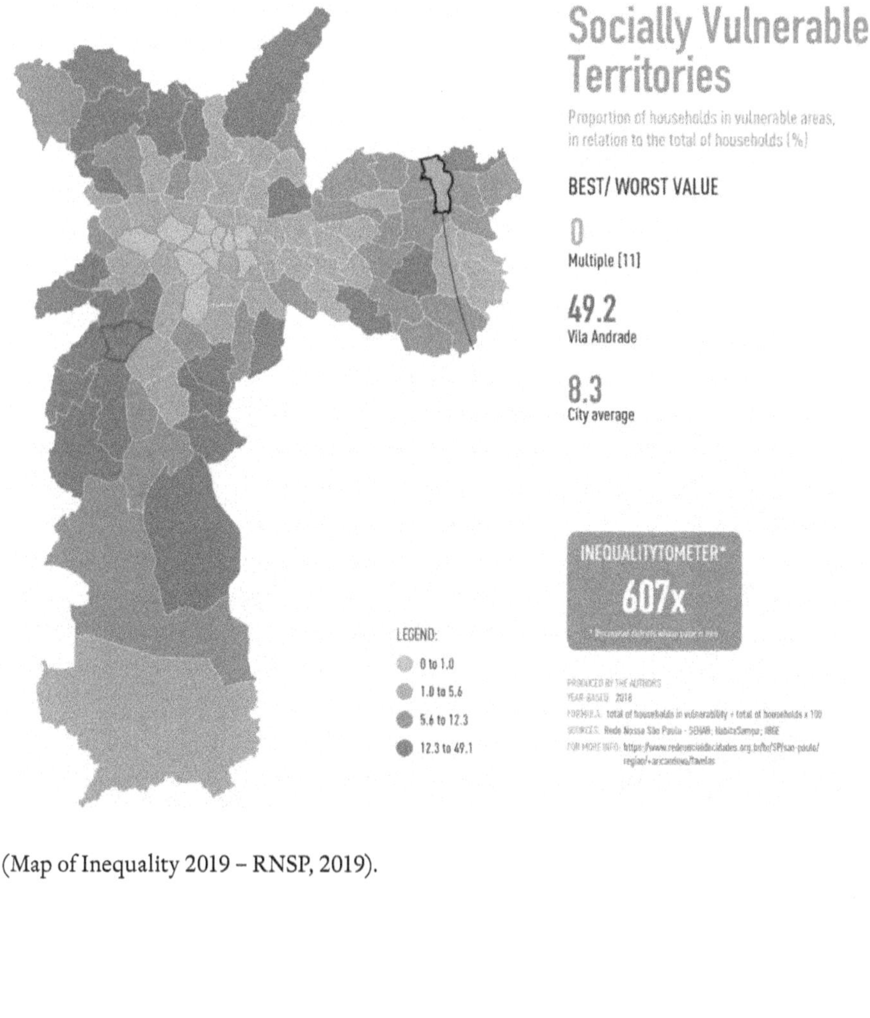

(Map of Inequality 2019 – RNSP, 2019).

FIGURE 2. **Map of Inequality showing the disparity in life expectancy in the districts of Moema (highest age expectancy at 80.6 years old) and in the district of Cidade Tiradentes (only 57.3 years old) and the average for the city of São Paulo is 68.7 years.**

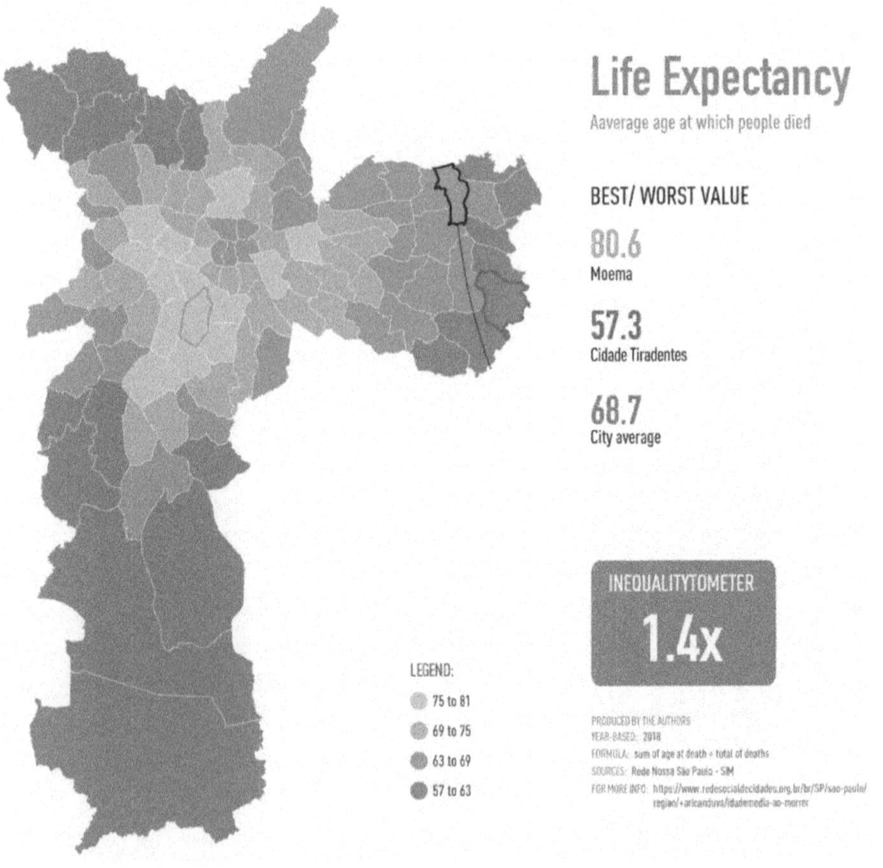

(Map of Inequality 2019 –RNSP, 2019).

Figures 1 and 2 illustrate some of the social inequalities found in São Paulo. In contrast to the central areas, the outskirts of the city have a high rate of social vulnerability that unfolds, among other factors, in life expectancy. The reinvention of coexistence in cities cannot be effective if social-spatial disparities prevail. The fact is that knowing this reality brings us to the necessity of transforming these territories, which requires innovative forms of urban planning.

Despite the emergence of important public policies that aim to promote the construction of a fairer and more sustainable urban environment, such as the City Statute([9]) and the Metropolis Statute([10]), the lack of integration between sectoral policies and the discontinuity of projects and policies have systematically harmed the transformation of Brazilian cities and neglected the local scale. Given this reality, which is not exclusive to Brazilian cities, the need arises to think of new forms of design, management and governance that work in an integrated manner, from a local perspective, that values and engages the population in this process.

5. Integrated local urban plans and incremental social urbanism

Some experiences in Latin America, although in progress and limited, shed light on the possible new paths and perspectives for the transition of urban peripheries toward resilience.

The reformulation of urban development and land policies in the city of São Paulo gained important progress with the 2014 Plano Diretor Estratégico – PDE (Strategic Master Plan). The PDE introduced new urban planning methodologies as well as innovative urban instruments, such as community participation and local urban plans. Notedly, such an advance occurred in the context of a sequence of challenges gradually tackled since the beginning of the new democratic process, with major achievements occurring during socially progressive governments and setbacks occurring during conservative governments.

A Latin American pioneer in the 1990s, Rio de Janeiro's Favela-Bairro program inaugurated a new approach to social and territorial inclusion through large-scale housing upgrading, developing specific programs for informal settlements that until then had been ignored by urban housing policies. In an incisive and innovative way, through unprecedented collaborative processes, it sought to improve the quality of life in informal

[9] The City Statute (Federal Law 10.257/2001) regulates "Urban Policy" the chapter of the Brazilian Constitution of 1988 (articles 182 and 183).

[10] The Metropolis Statute (Federal Law 13.089/2015.) establishes general guidelines for the planning, management and execution of public functions in metropolitan regions and in urban agglomerations.

settlements and transform them into neighborhoods integrated into the city. This pioneering case of improving territories of social vulnerability was implemented and has since been replicated in several cities and as national public policy in some countries, adapted to the specific conditions of each local context.

Such programs have consistently addressed the fundamental challenge of improving the quality of life in a number of informal settlements on the outskirts of the major cities in the region, mainly through the provision of basic infrastructure and affordable housing.

The programs start from the fundamental initial strategy of formally including informal settlements in the urban regulatory framework, and subsequently promoting quality participation in the development of local urban plans. Areas of environmental vulnerability, subject to landslides or flooding, as well as floodplain areas adjacent to streams, or at imminent risk of fire, are mapped and new housing is developed to replace the existing housing in these areas. Improvements to vehicle access for essential services (ambulances, fire trucks) are carried out through the settlements. The construction of basic infrastructure such as sanitation, water and energy supply, and sewage treatment systems is developed according to local possibilities and contexts. Public spaces are also built within the limited scope of existing vacant land and public facilities are installed (Leite et al., 2020).

Unfortunately, the Favela-Bairro program was interrupted after ten years, due to the serious and recurrent Brazilian and Latin American problem of the discontinuity of public policies and urban programs.

Other Latin American countries also underwent similar processes within the scope of the urban regulatory framework, as for example, the well-known and widely analyzed case of the urban planning process in the city of Medellín, Colombia (Leite et al., 2020).

The development of urban policies focusing on urban reform, as well as the utilization of urban planning instruments provided in federal laws are more evident in socially progressive municipal governments, where different forms of public policies, programs, plans, and urban interventions share the same core principles of social inclusion. The strategy of organizing urban development in a more inclusive way seeks to align local regulations and innovative urban instruments in order to produce concrete transformations within the territory in a continuous and incremental process of "social urbanism" (without miracles or quick solutions).

Social urbanism is therefore understood as an incremental urban development process. It presumes the existence of a strong, fully standardized, and democratic State that defines the rules for urban development with social participation and control, and where other private agents and civil society organizations are invited to act and assist in developing urban policies aimed at the construction of the city as a collective, democratic, and inclusive asset. This type of urbanism separates the ownership of the land from the right to build, the latter granted by the State; it aims to combat land and real estate speculation; it expands the use and access to public space, including the road system, favouring other modes of transportation in addition to individual car; prioritizes public investments, plus resources obtained via land value capture with a redistribution character; and guarantees ample transparency and a collaborative process in urban decision-making processes. (Leite et al., 2020).

There are no pre-established solutions that can be applied to all these social vulnerability areas. In some situations, regularization and urbanization are the appropriate paths to follow; in others, the best solution is the relocation of the residents to nearby housing developments, followed by the designation of the area for uses that prevent its reoccupation. But the imperative is the prior development of local urban plans that integrate and territorialize the different actions.

In São Paulo, favorable circumstances allowed local governments to adopt such an agenda, but the lack of continuity makes it difficult to consolidate social urbanism throughout the city. Although in a discontinuous way, different local governments have sought to implement these principles over the past years, generating relevant experiences (Getlinger, 2021).

Besides the experiences that come from public authorities and are related to regulatory frameworks, other initiatives aimed at promoting urban transformation in the peripheries have emerged from organized civil society itself in a bottom-up process. Many of them have shown promising results and boosted the urban transformation of peripheral territories, as is the case of the Pact for Fair Cities. (Getlinger, 2021).

The Pact for Fair Cities emerged in 2020 and aims to establish a new model of local urban governance and civic participation methodologies for urban interventions in socially vulnerable territories. For that, over

20 Non-Governmental Organizations (NGO), plus community and affordable housing organizations joined forces to expand the reach of civil society organizations and their capillarity in such areas, in a pioneering way to manage their social transformation assets. The pact also aims to integrate the experience of non-governmental entities already established in informal territories and in socially vulnerable territories with actions of the formal public sector in those areas (Pacto pelas Cidades Justas, 2020).

These initiatives have pointed out new and promising opportunities in the transition of some territories in the peripheries of São Paulo through an articulated set of actions that begin with (i) the process of urban land regularization, bringing to legal status the population that is in informality in territories of social vulnerability; (ii) the application of re-urbanization instruments; (iii) the promotion of urgent social housing and urbanization programs (support infrastructure, public equipment, public spaces).

The most promising novelty that emerged in 2019 with the initiative of the Pact for Fair Cities is the promotion in three peripheral territories of the city of Social Urbanism programs contemplating the following actions([11]):

- Integrated Local Action Plans;
- Integrated and locally territorialized public policies;
- Innovative shared governance: government, civil society, academia;
- Articulation of strategic, systemic, and local actions;
- Local anchor equipment / urban references;
- Tangible and intangible actions;
- Capacity-building for local community managers;
- Construction of data methodology and monitoring indicators;
- Application of the theory of change and formulation of integrated guidelines.

[11] New methodological work recently developed in São Paulo concerning incremental social urbanism in three specific socially vulnerable territories in the peripheries of the city and "Theory of Change as a tool to develop vulnerable territories" could be checked in: - https://www.cidadesjustas.org.br (access in 25/10/2021);- https://pp.nexojornal.com.br/ponto-de-vista/2021/Teoria-de-Mudança-como-instrumento-para-desenvolver-territórios-vulneráveis (access in 25/10/2021).

6. Concluding remarks

There is worldwide consensus that among the greatest challenges of the contemporary urban world are the territories of high social vulnerability where millions of poor people are anonymously left at the margins of society (UN-Habitat and World Health Organization 2020). Moreover, it has been widely argued in many academic and institutional circles that coexistence in cities cannot be effective if social-spatial disparities prevail. In such a dire scenario, especially after the outbreak of the Covid-19 pandemic, participatory urban planning arises as one of the best contemporary instruments at hand to promote increasing public well-being.

The discussion addressed in this article presents some fundamental elements that, taken as a whole, point to the sustainable evolution of an innovative incremental social urbanism process that is emerging in some territories pointing out a transition in peripheries. Using urban strategies that aim to activate spatial and social capital might bring high economic, social, and ecological benefit for all, – if activated and supported by innovative projects and new policies. This creativity of activation can contribute to a better use of local resources and be a basis for an ecological and social transition.

Tackling these problems – in a propositional, consistent, incremental, and continuous way, based on integrated and territorialized public policies, with their corresponding strategic, systemic, and local actions – is the inescapable challenge faced by São Paulo's transitioning peripheries in the emergence of the post-pandemic urban scenario. It requires innovative and shared governance models in which the valorization of democracy, ethics, science and transparency, and the willingness to serve society by performing the common good – the primary reason for the art of politics – underlie proposals and, especially, rigorously planned actions.

References

Bennett J., Belshaw C. (1976). The Ecological Transition. Oxford, Pergamon.

Barca F., McCann P., Rodriguez-Pose A. (2012) "The Case For Regional Development Intervention: Place-Based Versus Place-Neutral Approaches". In: Journal of Regional Science. 52(1) 2012. pp. 134–152.

Blundell R., Costa Dias M., Joyce R., Xu X. (2020) "COVID-19 and Inequalities". In: Fiscal Studies. Vol. 41, No. 2. pp. 291–319.

Getlinger, Daniela C. Vianna. Plano de ação local como elemento de integração e territorialização de políticas públicas em áreas de vulnerabilidade social: o caso do Jardim Lapena. Doctoral thesis. Faculty of Architecture and Urbanism of Mackenzie Presbyterian University. São Paulo, 2021.

IBGE. Instituto Brasileiro de Geografia e Estatistica. (2011) Censo Demográfico 2010. Aglomerados Subnormais. Primeiros Resultados. Rio de Janeiro, IBGE. Available at: https://biblioteca.ibge.gov.br/visualizacao/periodicos/92/cd_2010_aglomerados_subnormais.pdf. Access on April 10th, 2019.

IBGE. Instituto Brasileiro de Geografia e Estatistica. (2010) Censos Demográficos, 1940- 2010. Rio de Janeiro, IBGE.

Leite, Carlos et al. (2020) Social Urbanism in Latin America: Cases and Instruments of Planning, Land Policy and Financing the City Transformation with Social Inclusion. Springer, Cham. https://doi.org/10.1007/978-3-030-16012-8.

Lefebvre, H. (1967) Le droit à la ville. Paris, editions Anthropos.

Lino, B. (2018) "In-Transition Processes". In: Schröder J., Carta M., Ferretti M., Lino B. eds. (2018) Dynamics of Periphery. Atlas of Emerging Creative and Resilient Habitats. Berlin, Jovis. pp. 96–99.

Matthey, L. (2014) Building up stories: Sur l'action urbanistique à l'heure de la societe du spectacle integre. Geneva, A-Type.

Moulaert, F., Martinelli, F., Swyngedouw, E., Gonzalez, S. (2005) "Towards Alternative Model(s) of Local Innovation". In: Urban Studies 42/2005, pp. 1969-1990.

Pacto pelas Cidades Justas. (2020) Pacto Pelas Cidades Justas. 2020. https://cidadesjustas.org.br.

Pasternak, S.; Bogus, L. Favela em números. In: Alvim, A. T. B.; Rubio, V. M. (Ed.) Sustentabilidade em projetos de urbanização de assentamentos precários no Brasil: contextos, demandas e perspectivas. Barueri: Manole, 2022. p. 71-98.

Pasternak, Suzana; D'ottaviano, Camila. (2016) Favelas no Brasil e em São Paulo: avanços nas análises a partir da Leitura Territorial do Censo de 2010. Cadernos Metrópole, v. 18, p. 75-100.

Rede Nossa São Paulo- RNSP. (2019) Map of Inequality 2019. p 26. Available at: https://www.nossasaopaulo.org.br/wp-content/uploads/2019/11/Mapada_Desigualdade_2019_apresentacao.pdf. Access on September 15th, 2020.

Rose-Redwood R., Kitchin R., Apostolopoulou E., Rickards L., Blackman T., Crampton J., Rossi U., Buckley M. (2020) "Geographies of the COVID-19 pandemic". Dialogues in Human Geography. Vol. 10(2). pp. 97–106.

Scaffidi F., Lopez Franco M., Mottee L., Sharkey M. (2019) The role of activist researchers in urban and regional planning. In: AESOP 2019 Conference Proceedings. pp. 311-323.

Sennett R. (2018) Building and Dwelling: Ethics for the City. New York. Farrar, Straus and Giroux.

Schröder J., Carta M., Ferretti M., Lino B. eds. (2018) Dynamics of Periphery. Atlas of Emerging Creative and Resilient Habitats. Berlin, Jovis.

Schröder J., Carta M., Scaffidi F., Contato A. eds. (2021) Cosmopolitan Habitat. A Research Agenda for Urban Resilience. Berlin, Jovis.

Tock, F.; Lazzarini, S.; Vasconcelllos, L.; Setter, G. Teoria de Mudança como instrumento para desenvolver territórios vulneráveis. São Paulo: NEXO Jornal, 2021 (access in 20/10/2021).

UN-Habitat and World Health Organization. (2020) Integrating Health in Urban and Territorial Planning: A Sourcebook. 1st ed. Geneva: UN. https://www.who.int/publications/i/item/integrating-health-in-urban-and-territorial-planning.

8. URBAN PROJECTS *VS.* REAL ESTATE OPERATIONS: ABOUT DOCK *(DIQUE)* 1 IN PUERTO MADERO, BUENOS AIRES

Eunice Helena S. Abascal
Natalia Feld
Alicia Novick
Angélica Tanus Benatti Alvim

The photo of Dock 1 (Dique 1) in Puerto Madero shows a series of high--rise buildings that change the skyline of Buenos Aires, whose morphology does not fit into the scheme of sectors and axes of the 1989 Master Plan. Initially, the site was intended to be a trade fair and convention center, but through a change of uses and constructability, it became a great opportunity for real estate development. This new landscape found the conditions for this possibility in the approval of a change of uses and land subdivision, resulting from from a series of reinterpretations of existing regulations. This text focuses on the study of this process of building and regulatory transformation, which, we argue, allows us to contribute to recent debates on Large-Scale Urban Projects (*Grandes Proyectos Urbanos* – GPU), by examining the role of planning and management instruments and the network of actors operating – with unequal resources and interests – in the processes of territorial transformation.

In order to discuss this issue, it is useful to briefly recall the alternatives for the operation of Puerto Madero in Buenos Aires. In 1989, in a context of a change of government, economic crisis and monetary hyperinflation, the – Corporación Antiguo Puerto Madero SA (CAPMSA) was organized as the first public company under private law in the country to take charge of the repurposing of the 170 hectares of the city's old port. Like other Waterfront operations around the world, the initial project aimed to revitalize and expand the city center, recovering underutilized plots of land in a privileged location. Simultaneously, other concurrent interventions aimed at improving and expanding the center were being these included the Avenida de Mayo Revitalization Program and the Avenida de Mayo Rehabilitation Plan, based on social development and historical heritage programs, and the revaluation of buildings of heritage value for social housing, such as the Manzana de San Francisco, with the incorporation of the figure of historical protection areas – HPA (APH, in its Spanish acronym). The controversial process that went from the Master Plan to its materialization was very short, and if in the nineties it was seen as a model intervention, due to the quality of its project and innovations in management, later interpretations were extremely critical.

As in other Large-Scale Urban Projects, the study of its forms revealed those logics of urbanalización in the terms of Francesc Muñoz (2008), typical of certain internacionalized urban renewal landscapes and was visualized as a clear territorial expression of globalized capitalism (Lungo, 2005; Carmona, 2005; Smolka & Lungo, 2005; Cuenya, 2009; Vainer et al., 2012). The experience of Puerto Madero, was examined from the alternatives of the projective process (Etulain, 2009; Novoa, 2005) and from the singularity of the new model of public-private management, condensed in the network of actors and in the figure of the Corporation (de Gopegui, & Nuñez, 1996) that, later it was established as a 'model' that was transferred to other cities (Leite et al., 2020; Jajamovich, 2019; Rosentein et al., 2016; Silvestre & Jajamovich, 2020). In contrast, it was examined in association with neoliberal policies, as an instance of the territorialization of globalized capitalism (Corral, 2010; Cuenya & Corral, 2011; Rodriguez, 2020). In broad terms, critical studies interpreted the implementation of Large-Scale Urban Projects in general, and Puerto Madero in particular, as the subordination of local governments and agencies to the interests of private capital in line with the principles of urban entrepreneurialism. Thus, the planning and management instruments associated with the projects were viewed as a "laissez-faire" alternative while proposing some, few and insufficient, redistributive actions – such as the recovery of urban capital gains or public spaces ceded by developers to the city. The texts gathered in the recent book by Cuenya, Elinbaum and Ziccardi (2020) are illustrative of this perspective. In that key point, the transformations of Puerto Madero's Dock 1 were also an object of study that was privileged by Cuenya and Corral (2010; 2011), who review the relationship established between the process of purchase and sale of the lots and the consequent progressive valorization of the land. In this context, the Corporation was analyzed as an instrument that guaranteed the public-private partnership and was criticized for having favored real estate developers without having promoted policies for the redistribution of the resources obtained. These studies have the capacity to shed light on many aspects of the problem, from the macro-scale explanations, which see these interventions as a result of the new logics of globalized capitalism; however, they leave many questions in the shadows. First, due to historical circumstances, the context of the 1990s differs, in terms of financing, from that of the 21st century. Puerto Madero and Dock 1 are being dealt with in very different contexts. Secondly, we believe it is necessary to consider the dilemmas of the design itself – the specificity of the territory, the design guidelines, the relationship between the proposal and the built city, typical of the premises of urban projects. In the same direction, thirdly, it is necessary to contemplate the network of public and private actors involved, which is not identical in all places. This intermediate level is valued by transnational studies, interested in circulation processes and, more specifically, in the local impact resulting from global processes (Healey, 2013).

From this perspective, we propose to focus on the processes, giving an account of the proposal, the related instruments and the network of actors behind the conditions of plausibility and the implementation of the operation of Dock 1. Plans, norms, ordinances are the "instruments" through which the modalities of production of the territory are legitimized. In the case of Dock 1, the conditions of execution established by the Master Plan were transformed in the heat of negotiations, disputes and more or less opaque procedures. Is it an Urban Project, with the associated attributes, or is it a real estate development? As a preliminary hypothesis, we are interested in showing that, although Puerto Madero had components of an Urban Project, the operation of Dock 1 was simply a real estate operation, lacking the attributes of the concept.

The first section, "Notions and concepts", reviews the scope of "urban project" and "large-scale urban projects" in order to locate our object of study and specify the attributes of the concept. Next, in "The illusion: articulation as an execution strategy" we propose to analyze the beginning of the Puerto Madero Operation, viewed as a possibility of generating instances of articulation and consensus. The third section, "From bidding to construction: the keys to speculation", presents a proposal to restore the process that Dock 1 went through and the role assumed by the instruments, as negotiation areas between public and private actors. Finally, in "Actors-Strategies: what is public dilutes in the face of the private" we propose to account for the dissolution of these instruments in the face of the new strategies of the development companies that are beginning to operate in the context of the new century.

It should be noted that this text presents a series of provisional materials and hypotheses that require further elaboration.

Notions and concepts

In broad terms, it is possible to consider three moments, more superimposed than successive, during which the idea of "urban project" was formulated and transformed.

At the end of the 1960s, there was a first moment which can be called *experimentation and characterization*, when it was presented as an innovative instrument, in counterpoint with previous practices, in particular with the urban plans of the second post-war period. Novick, A. (2012). *Proyectos urbanos y otras historias.* SCA/Nobuko. In a profound context of paradigm change, the "urban project" (UP) was presented together with keywords of those years, such as "participation", "decentralization", "cultural heritage", "public space". The project thus conceived was tributary of the experiences that began with the morphologism and urban analysis developed in Italy based on the Architecture of the City to solve the problems of urban centers. By dealing with fragments of the city, as opposed to the great technocratic plans, implied a modest attitude, which promoted the recovery of intermediate scales, pondering the logics of historical processes and the realities of the inherited city (to respect, to dialogue, to ignore), while considering inertias, resistances and identities. From this perspective, it was an important part of what we call the "celebration of the fragment". This perspective that was in line with the "management by projects" of political science, which aimed at transforming urban administration by considering a conception of the social process that took into account the actors who, from different resources and strategies, intervene on the territory, in instances of requalification and negotiation[1].

In this framework, the notion of UP is ambiguous, but "a notion that is not fully clarified, that is neither too early nor too mechanically precise, when it comes against the grain of previous practices, is more productive in experiences and reflections than if it is fixed within the corset of imposed procedures", Marcel Roncayolo (1996: p. 67) affirmed. Precisely, the interest of the notion of urban project, even if it has caused fluctuations, resides in the kind of liability it introduces in the construction of cities and in the redefinition of spaces. The territory, the built space of the city was the initial condition and its transformation was the result. Nevertheless, these "first generation" UPs were the object of study where questions about forms and configurations prevailed, being also a renewed entry of architects to urban planning, which they recovered as urbanism. Most of the studies focused on the dilemmas of configurations and design solutions.

In a second moment, the notion was associated, almost without mediation, with those of "opportunity" since, as part of the strategic plans of the nineties, they are closely related to globalization and neoliberal policies. In this framework, they are incorporated, together with the lexicon of the business world, with terms such as "competitiveness", "competition", "public-private partnerships", and "marketing" when the new market referentials prevailed. Within a new generation of planning ideas, the plan had to ensure the strategic guidelines in a complementary way with a portfolio of projects of different scales, which could be materialized in the short, medium and long terms. Novick, A., & Feld, N. (2021). Territorios: Proyecto. *SI+ Palabras Clave. Conceptos, Términos, Metadatos*. Many of these guidelines were adopted by local governments as forms of action, generally in concertation with the private sector, acting on the urban reality. The

[1] A wide literature has tried to define the scope of the urban project and to systematize the experiences carried out. Mangin and Panerai, (1991) Devilliers (1994), condense the perspectives of architects who had very early defined the morphological typology as an operative instrument. From the management perspective, Toussant and Zimmerman (1998), who rescue the projects from the procedures for civil servants, how to promote participative methods, etc. All these French authors, give account of their specificity of thinking urban management and the articulations with sociology and anthropology that since Henri Lefevre and Manuel Castells, crossed by the experiences of May 68 are present in the ways of thinking the city. Sainz Gutierrez, (2006), Ingallina, (2008) refer to the experience in Spain and Italy.

idea was to loosen the set of regulations, formalities and public control which, it was assumed, hindered the possibility of carrying out interventions of a transforming and revitalizing nature, capable of increasing the city's attractiveness and competitiveness.

The UPs were thus instruments of valuation and resources for large--scale operations, giving rise to enormous uncertainty in differentiating a UP, whose impact qualifies the city as a whole and benefits urban society, from a real estate operation, whose objective is private profitability. Along these lines, the Large-Scale Urban Projects, a term used in France for the major interventions of the early 1980s and extended to large-scale operations, have been the object of criticism in Latin American literature. In the study of these "second generation" Large-Scale Urban Projects, two approaches prevailed, the celebratory ones, but, above all, the criticism that, from a macro perspective, analyzed them as a product of the new modes of territorialization of globalized capitalism, which we will examine in depth in the next chapter.

In a third moment, when the gaze of the city shifted to the territory, along with the new century, the idea of "territorial project" was consolidated, and currently coexists with "urban projects". Although they are not the subjects of this paper, it seemed important to mention their scope. The renewed planning context made it possible to think about the reincorporation of "territory in the agenda". The word "reincorporation" recalls that the problems of habitat, uncontrolled sprawl and lack of facilities had been the subject of the regional plans of the second post--war period, which proposed zoning, land use or infrastructure layouts to control growth and rebalance the modes of occupation. Novick, A. (2012). Los proyectos territoriales en perspectiva. In *Planes, proyectos e ideas para el AMBA* (pp. 35–47). CPAU. However, with regard to the problems of urban sprawl, the twenty-first century has brought many different scenarios and methodologies: how to understand these territories when the conceptual and operational tools available are inadequate, and how to recognize their specificity? Some recent experiences provide answers: unlike zoning and generic solutions typical of the regional plans of the past, the intentional reading of the territory, together with the capacity to project, are presented as key tools for knowledge and intervention.

In synthesis, the history of the term refers us to the temporalities of a notion, which was transformed along with the experiences that were formulated and materialized. Certainly, the macroeconomic, political and social dimensions configure the spaces of the capitalist city, nevertheless, there is a material specificity, constitutive of the notion of UP, and a specific need of knowledge resulting from the project activity that is convenient to consider in order to advance in the understanding of the logics that govern it.

The illusion: articulation as an execution strategy

From this brief genealogy of the notion of UP and its scope, it is possible not only to situate the process that Puerto Madero went through from its beginnings, in the epistemological debates of each moment, but also in the analytical perspectives that the bibliography used to study it.

In fact, the first reflections on alternatives for Puerto Madero were developed in line with the urban policy deployed in the 1990s, aimed at revitalizing the downtown area of the city through various programs. This policy was developed in a context of profound transformation in the relationship established between the new logics of capital circulation and the dynamics of territorial transformation. Large volumes of capital were poured into the transformation of space, as a result not only the economic process that characterized the 1990s and the spread of credit, but also of the introduction of a set of instruments related to the process of capital funding, introduced through the Housing and Construction Financing Law No. 24,441 (Clichevsky, 2001). This meant, especially in the second half of the decade, a strong increase in direct private investment in this sector, which began to have high profitability percentages. At the same time, this process was accompanied by the incorporation of new construction technologies and, therefore, of new real estate typologies such as shopping malls, supermarkets, "intelligent" buildings and high-rise construction. During this moment, called by Peresini (2019) "flexibilization and openness", the institutional bases were laid for public--private articulation from instances of consultation, legitimized from the principles of strategic planning in urban management. In this context, Puerto Madero began to take shape, especially from the possibility of, from a set of open programs and concrete actions, capitalizing on these new private investments to operate on the whole city from a fragment. The project was seen as an opportunity to implement two strategies. On the one hand, from the possibility of articulation with private capital, to guarantee the resources required for its realization and, on the other hand, from the recovery of the symbolic and material values of the traditional city, to build consensus for its implementation.

In this section, we propose to reinstate the process by which Puerto Madero went from the project debates to the instruments required for its implementation.

The beginning of this process is situated in November 1989, when the agreement for the creation of the Puerto Madero Corporation (*Corporación Puerto Madero*). Its goal was to unify the multiplicity of domains that intervened on the lands of Puerto Madero and simultaneously "guaranteeing the fulfillment of the political and urbanistic objectives of the Project" (Garay, 2002: 7). The Corporation was presented as the organizational instrument[2] capable of articulating the different levels of State that had jurisdiction over Puerto Madero (Federal and City of Buenos Aires) and overlapping administrative domains (National Ports Administration, Argentine Railways and the National Grain Board). Above all, it allowed the deployment of new management alternatives based on the trust in private participation in order to guarantee the execution of the project given the scarcity of public resources.

The first strategy deployed by the Corporation was related to the need to define the morphological and project conditions of the operation. In the first instance, through the frustrated hiring of Catalan experts (Jajamovich, 2016a), then in the face of the resistance of the Society of Architects and the consequent rejection of the original project, which had as a corollary the National Competition of Ideas of 1991. In this way, it was possible to grant legitimacy to the process and build the consensus required for its realization. Reviewing the Competition's Rules allows us to situate the morphological and project conditions around which the consensus was built. Thus, reflections on the alternatives for the expansion of tertiary, recreational and sports activities; the preservation and recycling of heritage; road and railway infrastructure; accesses, services and landscape design, among others, were incorporated into the "Program's Foundation". These are those attributes of the urban project

[2] Organizational instruments that refer to the institutional framework behind a specific public policy. As an example, he cites organizational structures and coordination and cooperation structures (Velasco, 2007).

that are in turn, as analyzed in the previous section, considered constitutive of its instrumentation. As shown in Figure 1, these were projected in terms of public spaces, articulation with the existing city, land use and lot subdivision.

FIGURE 1: **Puerto Madero Contest Final Project.**

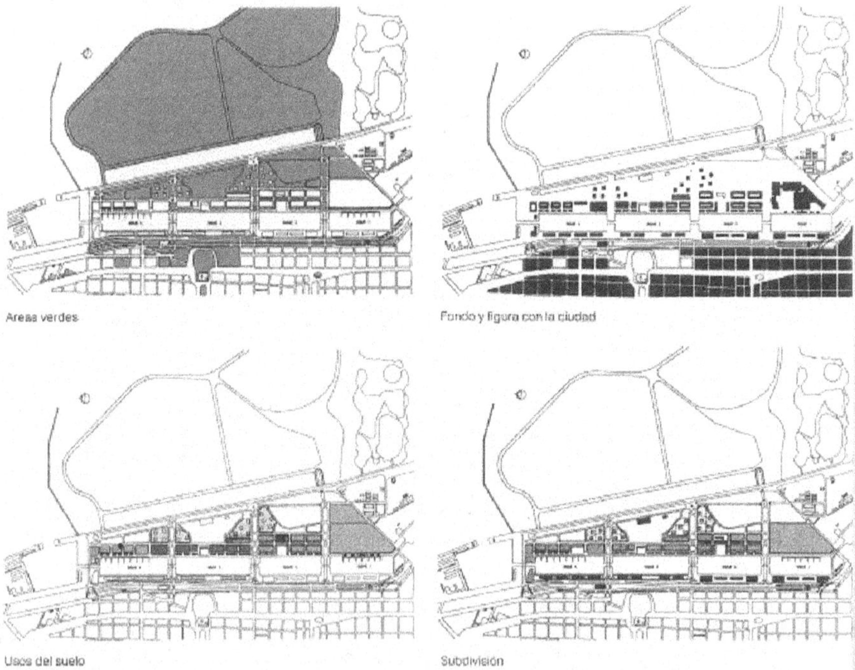

Source: Arquis (S/F) Old Puerto Madero Urbanization Contest (*Concurso de Urbanización Antiguo Puerto Madero*)

Once the competition process had been carried out and the general structure of the project had been approved, it was necessary to have the related instruments. In a context of tensions and disputes between the Planning Department and the Deliberative Council, the Corporation's strategy was to uphold the regulation in force (formulated during the military government), by which Puerto Madero was named U24 – special urbanization area (Garay, 2002). This established a generic FOS and FOT[3] for the whole sector without subdivisions and, therefore, made it possible to start the bidding and land allocation process without going through the political disputes that the approval of a new regulation in the Deliberating Council would entail.

Here, it is essential to bear in mind that the first steps in the management of the project were not only affected by the changes in the country's structural economic and financial conditions mentioned above, but also by the institutional character that the City acquired after the reform of the Argentine Constitution in 1994. Indeed, the autonomy acquired by the Government of the City of Buenos Aires had its correlate in a sort of return to the – strategic – urban planning. Particularly, the role assumed by the new Secretariat of Urban Planning impacted the Puerto Madero process on two dimensions. On the one hand, in the functioning of the Corporation's Board of Directors[4], which, since its composition, began to be affected by political-partisan disputes that had an impact on the modification of management criteria; In particular in the demands on the deadlines and conditions for the materialization of the projects (Garay, 2002). Secondly, the city government – now autonomous – proposed to incorporate the new "neighborhood" of Puerto Madero into the Urban Planning Code. This implied that the Urban Planning Council, and not the Corporation, would be the entity in charge of interpreting and applying the regulations. In this shift, two municipal departments, the Dirección de Planeamiento e Interpretación Urbanística and the Dirección General De Fiscalización De Obras y Catastro[5] (*Directorate of Urban Planning and Interpretation and the General Directorate of Construction Control and Cadastre*) became key players in the process.

In summary, in a context of strong changes in the relationship between capital and real estate investment, the Corporation deployed a series of

[3] FOS Soil Occupancy Factor; FOT – Total Occupancy Factor; number that multiplied by the total area of the plot determines the buildable area (CABA Ciudad Autónoma de Buenos Aires, Código de Planeamiento Urbano (Urban Planning Code), 2012).

[4] The Board of Directors of the corporation was initially composed of six appointed directors: four by the National Executive Power and the remaining two by the Mayor of the City of Buenos Aires. The presidency would rotate, the term of office was of one year and they acted ad honorem, as long as there are no genuine appeals (Article 4, Bylaws of Corporación Antiguo Puerto Madero S.A. Decree No. 1,279-PEN-89).

[5] From 1999 to 2002, they headed the Technical / Legal area of the Corporation Corporación Antiguo Puerto Madero S.A.

strategies that allowed it to build consensus around the attributes of the UP and to begin the bidding process for the Dams. However, the subsequent autonomy acquired by the City of Buenos Aires in 1994, modified the correlation of forces around the project's alternatives, opening new paths to interpretations guided more by the negotiation capacities of the developers than by the project conditions around which the consensus for its realization had been built. Thus, the shift in the meaning of UPs is being built, from complex interventions aimed at society and the city, to real estate developments.

From bidding to construction: the keys to speculation

The Puerto Madero operation, as we have shown, was presented as an alternative to stimulate the real estate market and expand the central area, without disregarding the premises of the UP that was conceived the area as part of the city. Within this framework, the Corporation consolidated itself as the Master Plan's enforcement authority, assuming the control and commercialization of the land, since it was an area that was not yet included in the guidelines of the City Planning Code. From that perspective, around the attributes of the Urban Project considered from the symbolic values of the port, the incorporation of new public spaces and the potential reactivation of the sector, the required consensus was built to start the bidding process for the docks. One of them, Dock 1, was destined for facilities and an exhibition center.

Now, how was the process by which this sector was transformed into a neighborhood of high-rise buildings? In this section, we examine the first stage of this transformation.

As early as the formulation of the Competition Rules, reflections on the need for a fairgrounds were incorporated: "the Corporation has already identified some investment interest in the construction of a fairgrounds whose main purpose would be the promotion of foreign trade (imports and exports)" (Rules for the Competition of Ideas for Puerto Madero, 1991, s. p). The regional scale of this facility was understood as a "favorable environment for the increase of foreign trade" (id., ibid.) within the framework of the recent creation of MERCOSUR. As can be seen in Figure 2, the Master Plan defined the location of this facility in Dock 1. To this end, the bidding terms defined as the object of the bid "(...) a complex basically intended for the exhibition, promotion and commercialization of products at regional, national and international levels with the activities typical of fairgrounds such as: exhibition center, convention center, hotel, communications, bank, insurance companies, etc. It was conceived as a "propitious environment for the increase of foreign trade" (CAPMSA, Terms and Conditions for the sale of real estate, 1992: 14). Thus, Dock 1 was classified as Special Facility (Equipamento Especial – EE).

FIGURE 2: **General outline of the Masterplan.**

Source: Puerto Madero Masterplan

FIGURE 3: **Masterplan land subdivision.**

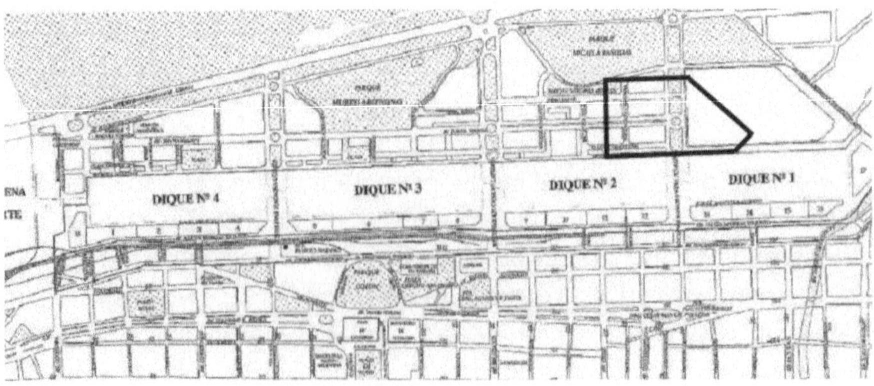

Source: CPAU Regulations (1989-2000)

The aforementioned particularities had their correlation in the bidding process and will be central in the subsequent evolution of the process. Firstly, as can be seen in Figure 3, the property was tendered as a whole/ unit, i.e. without internal layouts or subdivisions. Secondly, while the rest of the bids were made with two envelopes (one with the economic valuation of the proposal and another envelope containing the project and background information), Dock 1 was awarded exclusively with the economic valuation. In other words, at the time of the award, the development did not have an approved project.

Under these conditions, Dock 1 was awarded in 1993 to the company Newside S.A. which, under the name of Aranalfe, had experience in large scale developments from the development of Shopping Soleil and later Patio Bullrich, Alto Palermo, Galerías Pacífico, Shopping Liniers, Patio Olmos in Córdoba, Bulevar Shopping in Adrogué (Real Estate Report, 2007). However, the consolidation process of Dock 1 began in 2006, that is, 13 years after its bidding process. During this time, a series of factors took place that influenced the process by which the planned regional facilities materialized in a series of real estate developments without any degree of articulation and which totally ignored the guidelines established in the Master Plan that gave rise to them.

The first turning point occurred, as mentioned in the previous section, with the incorporation of Puerto Madero into the City's Urban Planning Code. This implied, among other things, the modification of the indicators that had been established in the Master Plan (Etulain, 2008).

In the case of Dock 1, the FOS went from 60% to 65% and the FOT from 1.7 to 3:

- " District 21- Section 98 – Block 1B – Dock 1 Area destined to the exhibition, promotion and commercialization of products on a national, regional and international level". Indicators: F.O.T. maximum: 3 F.O.S.: 65% Of the 65% allocated for the F.O.S. 57% may be used for buildings with maximum height = 29.50 m. and the remaining 8% for buildings with maximum height = 70 m.
- District 21 – Section 98 – Block 1A – Dock 1: "The construction of a parking lot below the level of the natural terrain shall be allowed. A park for public use shall be built on it, the work of which shall be paid for by the owner and shall include the development of its landscaping" (Urban Code, p. 535).

Here it is essential to take into account that within the foreseen indicators, 8% of the FOS was destined for buildings up to 70 m high. This definition will be central in the future disputes about the profitability expectations of future real estate developments, since other regulatory provisions changing the urbanization conditions would be published later on, modifying the process of lot sales.

The second turning point in the urbanization alternatives of Dock 1 can be situated in 1999 when, based on the request of Newside as the company awarded the Dock, a new plot structure was approved for Block 1B, without modifying the project norms. This process, which had begun with a Report from the General Directorate of Urban Planning and Interpretation (*Dirección General de Planificación e Interpretación Urbanística*), was approved through a Provision of the General Directorate of Construction Control and Cadastre (*Dirección General de Fiscalización de Obras y Catastro*) of the now Government of the City of Buenos Aires. Figure 4 shows the new plot structure, which, having been approved by Provision, was not submitted to the consideration of the City Legislature either.

FIGURE 4: **Surface area balance. New plot structure for Block 2B of Dock 1.**

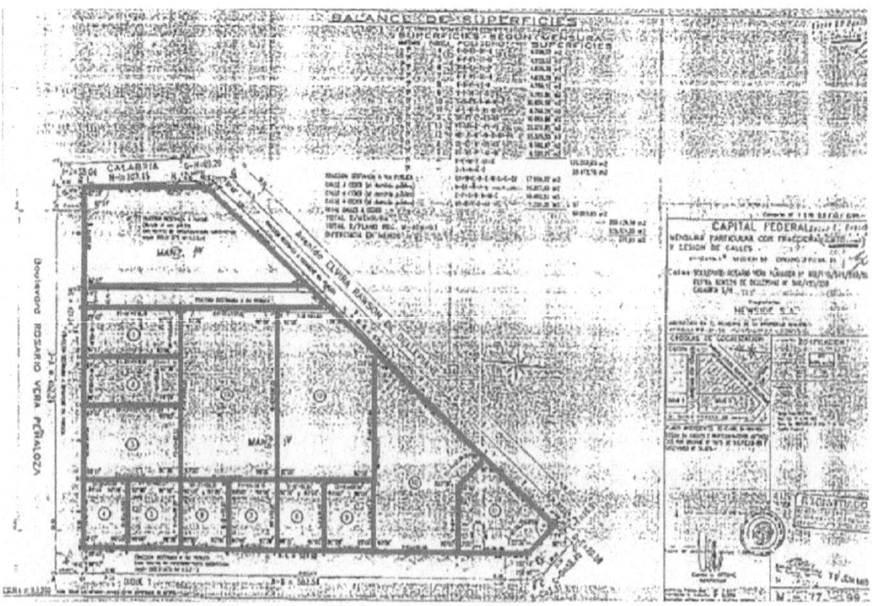

Source: Government of the City of Buenos Aires

The possibility of marketing the lots independently allowed Newside to consolidate its business strategy, which began with the inauguration that same year of the Malecon designed by the HOK (Martínez, 1999) International studio and the Aisenson studio (El Cronista. Arquitectura. Diseño & Decoración, 2/06/1999). This land, continuous to Dock 1, had been acquired by the company a few years earlier. Figure 5 shows the location of the development in relation to Dock 1, still vacant.

FIGURE 5: **Aerial view of the Malecon building developed by Newside, inaugurated in 2006.**

Source: Aisenson Studio. Retrieved from: http://asnnoise.com.ar/wp-content/uploads/expo--recoleta-catalogo-12-2006-1.pdf

However, in order to carry out its business strategy, Newside required, on the one hand, that those lots have a residential use (since they were still assigned the Special urban equipment use) and, on the other hand, the assignment of the urban indicators that would allow the commercialization of those lots. Once the new plot structure was approved, the disputes focused on defining the new uses and how the construction capacity of the initial lot was going to be distributed in the new plot structure. In this context, the controversial process was initiated through which the Directorate of Urban Planning and Interpretation approved a series of Provisions that granted the urbanization conditions necessary to begin the process of selling the lots.

The first one was Provision 310/99, which became famous as the "Prati Provision", which approved the distribution of the construction capacity assigned to the initial lot, according to the new plot structure. As mentioned in the previous section, the core of the dispute revolved around the distribution of 8% of the FOS that the Code allowed for the construction of 70 m high buildings in Dock 1. The legality of this Provision would later be questioned, not only because it was not published in the Official Gazette and therefore remained as a "not perfect" administrative act, but also because it contradicted the conditions established by the Urban Planning Code of the City.

Once the subdivision of the land and the urban indicators for each lot had been obtained, there was still the need to obtain the residential. For this purpose, the Directorate of Urban Planning and Interpretation approved two complementary provisions which, based on a "peculiar" interpretation of the Code, allowed Dock 1 to be reconverted to residential use. The first of these two provisions understood that the border on Vera Peñalosa Boulevard could have residential use because it was in front of Dock 2's residential area. The second one understood that, since according to the Building Code, Dock 1 was authorized for hotel use and Newside's real estate projects were condominiums with "hotel and amenities" services, these could be considered "Transitory Residence Units" and be assimilated to hotel use (which was contemplated). Both provisions allowed Newside to start marketing the lots in a context of high demand for the construction of premium real estate products. This management scheme by means of Provisions was the Municipality's strategy so that the modifications (new plot structure, FOS-FOT and change of uses) did not have to go through the disputes of the political arenas of the Deliberating Council. Figure 6 shows the impact, in terms of projects, of the approved regulations for Dock 1.

FIGURE 6: **General urbanization of Puerto Madero with the change of plot structure and uses of Dock 1.**

Source: Urban Development Master Plan for Puerto Madero. Extracted from https://www.modernabuenosaires.org/proyectosurbanos/plan-maestro-de-desarrollo-urbano-para-puerto-madero

In summary, the restitution of the process through which the instruments used for Dock 1 went through made it possible to identify the relevance acquired by the norm as an object of negotiation and dispute among the multiplicity of interests at stake. On the other hand, it made it possible to show that interpretation was used as a resource of exception in the process through which Dock 1 gradually lost the attributes of the project and consolidated as the fragmentation of the fragment. In other words, throughout the negotiation, the company established its own rules, without having the Administration enforce the rules and forms of the master plan, to which the proposal should have been adjusted.

Actors – Strategies: what is public dilutes in the face of the private

Up to this point it was possible, from the restitution of the process undergone by the instruments, to account for the way in which the initial project reflections on Dock 1 were redefined in the heat of the context conditions and the profitability demands of the developer for the commercialization of the new lots. This section questions the factors that influenced the process through which, once the required interpretations of the regulations were obtained, Newside implemented its business strategy, which in turn was affected by the new structural conditions of the context.

As described in the literature (Socoloff, 2019a; Raspall, 2018), approximately between 2000 and 2013, the country went through a strong reactivation process of the real estate market. This can be explained, on the one hand, as a consequence of the production surplus of the agro--export market and, on the other hand, because as a result of the distrust in the banking system, the class with higher purchasing power began to invest in the real estate sector, which was starting to show high levels of profitability. In turn, between 2006 and the international crisis of 2008, this process was deepened by the return of international companies that had withdrawn during the 2001 crisis. Subsequently, as of 2012, but more deeply as of 2014, the real estate market began to decline in the face, first, the restrictions for the acquisition of dollars and, then, the reduction of surplus flows from the agro-export market. In this context, large development companies began to deploy new intervention strategies to sustain the profitability of their developments, especially from the corporate organization (Peresini, 2019).

However, beyond the contextual conditions, one of the factors that restricted the possibility of starting to market the lots was related to the judicial litigation involving Dock 1. The company Newside, initially formed by Roberto Goldfarb and Jorge Ginevra, had close commercial ties with Banco Mayo. According to journalistic sources, part of the funds committed by Banco Mayo were used by Newside for the acquisition of Dock 1 (Pagina 12, 2005). This bank, whose president was Rubén Beraja, had initiated the bankruptcy process in October 1998 and in the context of the disputes surrounding the bankruptcy process, Federal Judge Norberto Oyarbide prohibited innovations on those lands until the conflict was solved.

This process was partially resolved in August 2005, opening a new stage of negotiations and agreements regarding the commercialization and destination of the Dock 1 land. From that moment on, Jorge Ginevra ceased to be a partner of Goldfarb, reorganized the structure of Newside and changed its name to GNV Group. Under this name, the process of commercialization of the lots would begin. The first was Plot 10 acquired by Desarrolladora G y D, then formed by Daniel Mintzer and Gabriel Mayo.

Subsequently, both companies, GNV Group (formerly Newside) and GyD, started a litigation process about the way in which Provision 310/99 had distributed the construction capacity of the original plot in the new plot structure. The dispute revolved around the distribution of eight percent (8%) of the FOS for the construction of towers of up to 70 m mentioned in the previous section. The conflict began when GyD, once it had acquired the land for the development of the project called +5411, disregarded Provision 310/99 and demanded that the entire 8% be applied to its land. Regarding this dispute, it was understood that if the 8% was granted to GyD, the percentage of towers would be restricted to GNV Group for the development of Madero Harbour on plots 12 and 13. In this regard, José Luis Villaveiran, vice-president of the developer, said:

> "We do not want to attack any project, but we do want 310/99 to be respected because it reflects the general order of the neighborhood and under which we created the Madero Harbour project, with 10.4% of the land for buildings up to 70 meters high. Under the Code this percentage would be reduced to 8%." (Perfil Newspaper, 2007, n. p.).

The resolution of this conflict and the way in which the percentage destined to towers would be distributed would be central in the future, not only of the land being developed by GyD and GNV Group, but also the commercialization alternatives for the rest of the land. Finally, the court disregarded Provision 310 and allowed GyD to carry out the planned real estate development. Once this dispute was resolved in 2008, the company sold plot 10 to the Crearurban Group (real estate developer of the Macri Group) who, with the new indicators approved, developed, on the basis of the +5411 project, the so-called Art María.

At the same time, GNV Group (formerly Newside) began to sell the rest of the lots in order to obtain the necessary capital for the development of the Madero Harbour project[6]. On the one hand, plots 4 and 5, which had been acquired by the construction company Skanka, were later resold in 2006 to Grupo IQ (Grupo Vidanta owned by Daniel Chávez Morán) for the development of the Mayan Resort Hotel and were finally purchased by Related Group owned by Jorge Pérez, for the construction of the project called SLS Lux Puerto Madero, which would be inaugurated in March 2020 (Jungle, 2020).

[6] "We bought the land with my dad in 1992. It was a bidding process from the National Government. At that time it was a single plot, with no services. Then it was divided into two and the larger one, in turn, was divided into 13 smaller plots. We had to do everything, get the feasibility... In the midst, my father died, the company was in debt and we had to sell part of it to Mayans (...) and also the land that Creaurban has today. Then we also sold another part to Banco Macro, whose partners Vizora and Fernández Prieto, undertook another project. Then we were able to raise capital to continue the work" (Reporte Inmobiliario (2010, p. 1).

On the other hand, in September 2005, the Trust "Madero 7" (abogados.com, 2011), whose majority owner was Vizora (a Banco Macro company presided by Jorge Brito) was created for the acquisition of five hectares distributed in plots 1, 2, 3, 6, 7, 8, 9 and 11 of Dock 1. Here it is necessary to take into account that Banco Macro Bansud had already offered to buy such plots on several occasions, and to pay a price that would allow the depositors to recover a good part of the money lost, and cancel other liabilities in the lawsuit for the bankruptcy of Banco Mayo mentioned above.

> "Due to its importance, the structure of the transaction constituted a milestone for the Argentine real estate market since it allowed raising funds from the capital market (both from local and foreign sources) in order to allocate them to the development of the real estate and construction activity and, consequently, to the financing of the real economy" (abogados.com, 2011, n. p.).

In 2007 (La Nación, 2007) Fernandez Prieto acquired 50% of the Madero 7 Trust (IProfesional, 2010) and began the development of the real estate projects. In 2009, the development of Zencity began in plots 1, 2 and 3. Subsequently, in 2015, the construction of Link Towers began in plots 8 and 9. Finally, in plot 11, the Trust developed a golf driving range and plots 6 and 7 have not yet been developed.

FIGURE 7: **Zencity development.**

Source: Eunice Abascal, 2019

FIGURE 8: **Pedestrian view of Dock 1.**

Source: Eunice Abascal, 2019

As can be seen in the images, these developments far exceed the 70 m height established by the Code for 8% of the FOS. At this point, it is worth noting that the developers obtained exceptions to the rule, based on the new profitability expectations. How did they achieve such benefits? It is important to recall the hypothesis that, if Puerto Madero had Urban Project components, the operation of Dock 1 was simply a real estate operation.

One possible answer lies in the corporate organization. Socoloff (2019b) identified as Financial Urban Coalition, constituted primarily by the Association of Housing Companies (AEV) but mainly by the Chamber of Urban Developers (CEDU). The latter includes the country's large development companies, some of which were developing Dock 1, such as G&D Developers, Vizora, FP Y Asociados, among others.

Particularly, in relation to Dock 1, the companies also formed the "Consorcio Dique 1" (Cronista. Impresa General, 2006) with the purpose of achieving an integrated urban development based on its own Master Plan. It was formed by the Trust Madero 7, GNV Group (formerly Newside), GyD and the Mexican company Mayan Resort.

> "We tried not only to coordinate uses, but also to harmonize volumes and create an internal law. Working together allowed us greater architectural freedom than our colleagues in the rest of the docks. The great difference that this area of Puerto Madero will have is that it will appear to the public as a whole designed as a whole, emphasizes Gabriel Mayo, general manager of G&D" (Cronista. Impresa General, 2006, p.1).

In summary, the process of acquisition and commercialization of Dock 1 made it possible to show that the complexity of these processes goes beyond the subordination of the State to private companies and that there are a series of factors, actors and temporalities that in different scales throughout the process that goes from the formulation of the project to the materialization of the developments. From this perspective it was possible to show that Dock 1 ceased to be a piece of the expanded project, proposed by the Master Plan, and became a set of real estate developments stripped of any possible attribute built around the notion of UP.

Closing remarks

In the introduction, we proposed to reflect on the relationship between the very notion of urban project from its attributes and the evolution of the process of consolidation of Dock 1. We also wondered about the relevance of the instruments in the configuration of the areas of dispute between the multiplicity of interests at stake and how these are settled around the correlation of forces resulting from its implementation.

In order to address these issues, it was central to take into consideration the scope of the notion of urban project in its ambiguities and mutations so as to, from the characterization of the three key moments, situate the first steps of Puerto Madero between the confidence in the fragment and private investment as an opportunity. Especially in the 90's, from the reinterpretation of the strategic planning model that, in relation to real estate development, was presented as a possibility to capitalize on private foreign investments that began to enter the country.

In a second moment, these attributes around which it was possible to build the consensus required for its implementation, began to blur in the face of the institutional rearticulation of land management, first as a result of the autonomy assumed by the city and secondly, the incorporation of Puerto Madero to the Planning Code.

Finally, during the last period, the conditions for implementation began to depend more on the negotiation capacities of the companies and less on the conditions of the Master Plan. In fact, the attributes of the very notion of UP, around which consensus had been built, were blurred in the face the development companies' new strategies and the institutional weaknesses of the Planning Secretariat.

Conceptually, the approach made it possible to show that the analysis of Large-Scale Urban Projects requires overcoming those assumptions that understand it as a product of the territorial anchoring of globalized capitalism and public agendas subjected to those interests. A look at the processes and instruments allow us to observe other complexities related to local political, economic and institutional conditions and the strategies deployed by companies to operate in areas of negotiation around which power relations are settled. Feld, N. (2021). Actores y procesos en los convenios urbanísticos para Puerto Norte en Rosario . Notas sobre lo público y lo privado. *Cuaderno Urbano*, 31, 9–34. To this end, it is essential to examine the processes that go from their formulation to their materialization, as they show the factors at play at different levels, as well as the multiple actors that, from their strategies and differential resources, intervene in the construction of the city. The relevance acquired by the multilevel approach lies in the possibility of simultaneously analyzing the macro level related to the new modes of production and consumption of globalized capitalism, but also from the micro level, in the local specificities resulting from the multiplicity of public and private interests that, crossed by political and ideological disputes, structure the network of actors behind them. In this way, it was possible to contribute new perspectives to the approaches based on the assumption that the private sector "manipulates" these instruments, and to show that these are processes that mobilize different levels of public administration.

Now, should every large-scale real estate development be studied and analyzed from the conceptual alternatives of the notion of the Urban Project? According to our perspective, this characterization does not apply to those operations where the attributes of the project are diluted and subordinated to the profitability logic of large developers who, as the literature suggests, evade all administrative controls.

Finally, this study, whose results are still provisional, shows the need to reflect on the role of projects in and on the processes of territorial transformation.

Bibliographic references

Abogados.com.ar. Bruchou, Fernández Madero & Lombardi – Abogados y Cárdenas, Di Ció, Romero & Tarsitano Asesoran en Financiamiento para el Mercado Inmobiliario Argentino. Available at: https://abogados.com.ar/bruchou-fernandez-madero-lombardi-abogados-y-cardenas-di-cio-romero-tarsitano-asesoran-en-financiamiento-para-el-mercado-inmobiliario-argentino/7436.

Carmona, M. (2005). Globalización y Cambios Conceptuales en el Desarrollo Urbano. Viejas Contradicciones y Nuevos Paradigmas. In M. Carmona & A. Arrese (Eds.), *Globalización y Grandes Proyectos Urbanos: La respuesta de 25 ciudades*. Infinito.

CABA Ciudad Autónoma de Buenos Aires, Código de Planeamiento Urbano, 2012. Available at: http://ssplan.buenosaires.gob.ar/documents/cpu2013/tomo%201.pdf.

Clichevsky, N. (2001). Mercado de tierra y sector inmobiliario en el Area Metropolitana de Buenos Aires – AMBA-.Transformaciones e impactos territoriales. *VI Seminario RII*.

Concurso de Urbanización Antiguo Puerto Madero. (S/F) Arquis. Available at: Available at: http://www.observatorioamba.org/descargas/adjuntos/memoria--plan-maestro.pdf

Corral, M. M. (2010). Neoliberalismo, Reformas Estructurales y Grandes Proyectos Urbanos: Estado y actores económicos en el Proyecto de Puerto Madero. *Intersticios: Revista Sociológica de Pensamiento Crítico*, *4*(2), 187–206.

Cronista. Impresa General (16/06/2006). El Banco Macro vendió en $ 47 millones su participación en Dique 1. Available at: https://www.cronista.com/impresa-general/El-Banco-Macro-vendio-en-47-millones-su-participacion-en-Dique-1-20060616-0091.html

Cronista. Impresa General (01/06/2006) +5411: el dique uno se pone a tono Available at: https://www.cronista.com/impresa-general/5411-el-dique-uno-se-pone-a-tono-20060601-0073.html

Cuenya, B., Elinbaun, P.; Ziccardi, A. (2020). Grandes Proyectos Urbanos. Conceptos clave y casos de estudio. Mexico DF, Universidad Nacional Autónoma de México.

Cuenya, B. (2009). Grandes Proyectos Urbanos Latinoamericanos. Aportes para conceptualizacion y gestion desde la perspectiva del gobierno local. *Cuaderno Urbano*, *8*(8), 229–252.

Cuenya, B., & Corral, M. M. (2011). Empresarialismo, economía del suelo y grandes proyectos urbanos: el modelo de Puerto Madero en Buenos Aires. *EURE (Santiago)*, *37*(1083), 25–45. Available at: http://www.scielo.cl/scielo.php?script=sci_arttext&pid=S0250-71612011000200002

Cuenya, B. (2020). Presentación. In B. Cuenya, P. Elinbaum, & A. Ziccardi (Eds.), *Grandes Proyectos Urbanos. Conceptos Clave y Estudios de Caso*. PUEC UNAM.

De Gopegui, G. R., & Nuñez, T. (1996). *Generacion de procesos urbanos: estrategias de lo publico y lo privado en el marco de una nueva cultura urbanistica: caso Puerto Madero*. Universidad de Belgrano, Investigacion de Alumnos, Programa de Iniciacion en la Investigacion.

Devilliers C. (1994). *Le Projet Urbain*. Paris, Ed. du Pavillon de l'Arsenal.

Diario Perfil (06/2007) Puerto Madero. Available at: http://www.diarioperfil.com.ar/edimp/0183/articulo.php?art=1792&ed=0183

El Cronista Arquitectura. Diseño & Decoración (2/06/1999) Edificio Malecom. En el sur, Mirando al Norte Available at: http://aisenson.com.ar/wp-content/uploads/2016/06/2009-08-12_12-10-37__Malecon-El-Cronista-06-1999-1.pdf.

Etulain, J. C. Gestión Promocional o privatización de la gestión urbanística? In: Universidad Nacional de Colombia, Bitacora 12, 2008. Available at: https://books.google.com.br/books?id=OB6-iN0C034C&pg=PA179&lpg=PA179&dq=dique+1+Puerto+Madero++y

______.(2009). *Gestión urbanística y proyecto urbano. Modelos y estratégias de intervención*. Buenos Aires, Nobuko.

Feld, N. (2021). Actores y procesos en los convenios urbanísticos para Puerto Norte en Rosario. Notas sobre lo público y lo privado. *Cuaderno Urbano*, 31, 9–34.

Gama Propiedades (2009). Alan Faena quiere construir nn Mega Hotel en Bariloche. Available at: http://gamapropiedades.blogspot.com/2009/12/alan-faena-quiere--construir-un-mega.html.

Garay, A. (2002). Acerca de la Gestión de proyectos urbanos: Las enseñanzas de Puerto Madero. In J. Liernur (Ed.), *Puerto Madero Waterfront: Vol. Case Nº 6*. Harvard University Graduare School of Desing, Prestel.

Gobierno de la Ciudad Autónoma de Buenos Aires – CABA (2018). Código Urbanístico. Anexo II Áreas Especiales Individualizadas. Buenos Aires, Subsecretaria de Planeamiento. Available at: https://www.buenosaires.gob.ar/sites/gcaba/files/codigo_urbanistico_anexo_ii_areas_especiales_individualizadas_0.pdf.

Gutiérrez, V. S. (2006). *El proyecto urbano en España: génesis y desarrollo de un urbanismo de los arquitectos* (Vol. 17). Universidad de Sevilla.

Healey, P. (2013). Circuits of knowledge and techniques: The transnational flow of planning ideas and practices. *International Journal of Urban and Regional Research, 37*(5), 1510–1526. Available at: https://doi.org/10.1111/1468-2427.12044

Ingallina, P. (2008). Le projet urbain, une notion floue. *Que sais-je?, 3*(3585), 7-13.

IProfesional (2010). Destinan u$s180 M para construir en el último terreno de Puerto Madero. Available at: https://www.iprofesional.com/notas/107097-puerto-madero-Destinan-us180-M-para-construir-en-el-ultimo-terreno-de-Puerto-Madero.

Jajamovich, G. (2016a). Historicizing the circulation of urban policies through career paths analysis: Barcelonian experts and their role in redeveloping Buenos Aires' Puerto Madero. *Iberoamericana, 18*(2010), 279–299. Available at: https://doi.org/10.18441/i

Jajamovich, G. (2016b). Puerto madero 'en movimiento': Movilidad de políticas y modelos urbanos en América latina(1999-2012). *Revista INVI, 31*(87), 59–84. Available at: https://doi.org/10.4067/invi.v0i0.950

Jajamovich, G. (2019). Grandes proyectos urbanos alternativos o alternativas a los grandes proyectos urbanos : una revisión a partir del concepto de just city Large Alternative Urban Projects or Alternatives to Large Urban Projects : A Revision on the basis of the Concept of Ju. *Cuadernos de Geografía: Revista Colombiana de Geografía, 28*(2), 394–407. Available at: https://doi.org/10.15446/rcdg.v28n2.72090.1

Jungle (11/03/20) Inaugura SLS en Puerto Madero. Available at: https://jungle.com.ar/inaugura-sls-en-puerto-madero/.

La Nación. El Banco Macro suma un socio para su proyecto en Puerto Madero. Available at: https://www.lanacion.com.ar/economia/el-banco-macro-suma-un-socio-para-su-proyecto-en-puerto-madero-nid874624/.

Leite, C., Acosta, C., Militelli, F., Jajamovich, G., Wilderom, M., Bonduki, N., Somekh, N., & Herling, T. (2020). Buenos Aires and Rosario: Large-Scale Urban Projects and the Just City. In *Social Urbanism in Latin America* (pp. 137–147). Available at: https://doi.org/10.1007/978-3-030-16012-8_6

Lungo, M. (2005). Globalización, grandes proyectos y privatización de la gestión urbana. *Urbano, 8*, 49–58. Available at: http://www.redalyc.org/pdf/198/19801107.pdf?origin=publication_detail

Mangin, O, Panerai, C. (1991). *Projet urbain*, Marsella: Parentheses

Martínez, S. (1999) Un nuevo símbolo de Puerto Madero. Arquinauta Año 1, Número 1. Available at: http://aisenson.com.ar/wp-content/uploads/2016/12/Malecon-Arquinauta-10-1999.pdf

Municipalidad de la Ciudad de Buenos Aires y Sociedad Central de Arquitectos. Bases para el Concurso de Ideas para Puerto Madero (1991). Available at: https://observatorioamba.org/descargas/adjuntos/memoria-plan-maestro.pdf.

Muñoz, F. (2008). *Urbanalización: paisajes comunes, lugares globales* (No. Sirsi) i9788425218736).

Novick, A. (2012a). *Proyectos urbanos y otras historias.* SCA/Nobuko.

Novick, A. (2012b). Los proyectos territoriales en perspectiva. *In Planes, proyectos e ideas para el AMBA* (pp. 35–47). CPAUd.

Novick, A., & Feld, N. (2021). Territorios: Proyecto. *SI+ Palabras Clave. Conceptos, Términos, Metadatos.*

Novoa, G (2005). Puerto Madero: un proyecto bisagra. En: Welch Guerra, M. Buenos Aires a la deriva. Transformaciones urbanas recientes. Editorial Biblos.

Página 12. La batalla por la última joya de Puerto Madero. Publicado en 05/05/2005. Available at: https://www.pagina12.com.ar/diario/economia/2-50612-2005-05-05.html

Peresini, N. (2019). *La institucionalización de Convenios Urbanísticos en la ciudad de Córdoba, Argentina. Un análisis de las adaptaciones normativas e institucionales en favor del proceso de neoliberalización en la gestión urbana local (1983-2019). ¿De las concertaciones a l.* Universidad Nacional de General Sarmiento.

Pliego de Bases y Condiciones para la venta de inmuebles. (1992) CAPMSA.

Raspall, T. (2018). Actores y estrategias empresarias en el mercado inmobiliario. Un análisis de la oferta de vivienda nueva en la ciudad de Buenos Aires durante los primeros años de la posconvertibilidad. *Cuaderno Urbano, 23*(23), 7. Available at: https://doi.org/10.30972/crn.23232687

Reporte Inmobiliario (11/06/2007) De Aranalfe a Newside Available at: https://www.reporteinmobiliario.com/nuke/article944-de-aranalfe-a-newside.html

Reporte Inmobiliario (18/08/2010) La Visión de los Ginebra Available at: https://www.reporteinmobiliario.com/nuke/article1612-la-vision-de-los-ginevra.html

Rodriguez, G. (2020). Grandes Proyectos, gentrificación y desplazamientos ¿Una relación necesaria? In B. Cuenya, P. Elinbaum, & A. Ziccardi (Eds.), *Grandes proyectos urbanos. Conceptos claves y casos de estudio.* PUEC UNAM.

Roncayolo, M. (1996). Conceptions, structures matérielles, pratiques. Réflexions autour du «projet urbain». *Enquête. Archives de la revue Enquête,* (4), 59-68.

Rosentein, C., Chajchir, E., Molteni, G., Formica, D., Ruani, J., & Ruani, S. (2016). Los grandes proyectos urbanos y la construcción de «lo público». El caso de la renovación de los frentes ribereños en ciudades argentinas. *Arquisur Revista, 9,* 134–145.

Sainz Gutierres, Victoriano (2006). El proyecto urbano en España: génesis y desarrollo de un urbanismo de los arquitectos. Sevilla, Universidad de Sevilla.

Silvestre, G., & Jajamovich, G. (2020). The role of mobile policies in coalition building: The Barcelona model as coalition magnet in Buenos Aires and Rio de

Janeiro (1989–1996). *Urban Studies*, *58*(11), 2310–2328. Available at: https://doi.org/10.1177/0042098020939808

Smolka, M., & Lungo, M. (2005). Tierra y grandes proyectos urbanos: una relación crítica. *ECA: Estudios Centroamericanos*, *678*, 379–384.

Socoloff, I. (2019a). Financiarización variada de la producción inmobiliaria en Argentina: el caso del boom inmobiliario en Buenos Aires y la postcrisis en perspectiva (2002-2015). *Scripta Nova*, *XXII* (616).

Socoloff, I. (2019b). Subordinate Financialization and Housing Finance: The Case of Indexed Mortgage Loans' Coalition in Argentina. *Housing Policy Debate*. Available at: https://doi.org/10.1080/10511482.2019.1676810

Toussant et Zimmerman (1998), *Projet urbain, menager les gens, amenager la ville*, Paris: Mardaga

Vainer, C., Oliveira, F. L. De, Novais, P. De, & Junior, L. (2012). Notas metodológicas sobre a análise de grandes projetos urbanos. In *Grandes Projetos metropolitanos: Rio de Janeiro e Belo Horizonte*. (pp. 11–23). Letra Capital.

Velasco, M. (2007). Distintos instrumentos para un mismo fin. Los instrumentos de las políticas públicas como herramienta para el análisis. *VIII Congreso Español de Ciencia Política y de La Administración*.